Pagan Portals
&
Shaman Pathways

...an ever-growing library of shared knowledge.

Moon Books has created two unique series where leading authors and practitioners come together to share their knowledge, passion and expertise across the complete Pagan spectrum. If you would like to contribute to either series, our proposal procedure is simple and quick, just visit our website (www.MoonBooks.net) and click on Author Inquiry to begin the process.

If you are a reader with a comment about a book or a suggestion for a title we'd love to hear from you! You can find us at facebook.com/MoonBooks or you can keep up to date with new releases etc on our dedicated Portals page at facebook.com/paganportalsandshamanpathways/

'Moon Books has achieved that rare feat of being synonymous with top-quality authorship AND being endlessly innovative and exciting.'
Kate Large, Pagan Dawn

Pagan Portals

Animal Magic, Rachel Patterson
An introduction to the world of animal magic and working with animal spirit guides

Australian Druidry, Julie Brett
Connect with the magic of the southern land, its seasons, animals, plants and spirits

Blacksmith Gods, Pete Jennings
Exploring dark folk tales and customs alongside the magic and myths of the blacksmith Gods through time and place

Brigid, Morgan Daimler
Meeting the Celtic Goddess of Poetry, Forge, and Healing Well

By Spellbook & Candle, Mélusine Draco
Why go to the bother of cursing, when a bottling or binding can be just as effective?

By Wolfsbane & Mandrake Root, Mélusine Draco
A study of poisonous plants, many of which have beneficial uses in both domestic medicine and magic

Candle Magic, Lucya Starza
Using candles in simple spells, seasonal rituals and essential craft techniques

Celtic Witchcraft, Mabh Savage
Wield winds of wyrd, dive into pools of wisdom; walk side by side with the Tuatha Dé Danann

Dancing with Nemetona, Joanna van der Hoeven
An in-depth look at a little-known Goddess who can help bring peace and sanctuary into your life

Fairy Witchcraft, Morgan Daimler
A guidebook for those seeking a path that combines modern Neopagan witchcraft with the older Celtic Fairy Faith

God-Speaking, Judith O'Grady
What can we do to save the planet? Three Rs are not enough. Reduce, reuse, recycle...and religion

Gods and Goddesses of Ireland,
Meet the Gods and Goddesses of Pagan Ireland in myth and modern practice

Grimalkyn: The Witch's Cat, Martha Gray
A mystical insight into the cat as a power animal

Hedge Riding, Harmonia Saille
The hedge is the symbolic boundary between the two worlds and this book will teach you how to cross that hedge

Hedge Witchcraft, Harmonia Saille
Learning by experiencing is about trusting your instincts and connecting with your inner spirit

Hekate, Vivienne Moss
The Goddess of Witches, Queen of Shades and Shadows, and the ever-eternal Dark Muse haunts the pages of this poetic devotional, enchanting those who love Her with the charm only this Dark Goddess can bring

Herbs of the Sun, Moon and Planets, Steve Andrews
The planets that rule over herbs that grow on Earth

Hoodoo, Rachel Patterson
Learn about and experience the fascinating magical art of
Hoodoo

Irish Paganism, Morgan Daimler
Reconstructing the beliefs and practices of pre-Christian Irish
Paganism for the modern world

Kitchen Witchcraft, Rachel Patterson
Take a glimpse at the workings of a Kitchen Witch and share in
the crafts

Meditation, Rachel Patterson
An introduction to the beautiful world of meditation

Merlin: Once and Future Wizard, Elen Sentier
Merlin in history, Merlin in mythology, Merlin through the
ages and his continuing relevance

Moon Magic, Rachel Patterson
An introduction to working with the phases of the Moon

Nature Mystics, Rebecca Beattie
Tracing the literary origins of modern Paganism

Pan, Mélusine Draco
An historical, mythological and magical insight into the God Pan

Pathworking through Poetry, Fiona Tinker
Discover the esoteric knowledge in the works of Yeats,
O'Sullivan and other poets

Runes, Kylie Holmes
The Runes are a set of 24 symbols that are steeped in history, myths and legends. This book offers practical and accessible information for anyone to understand this ancient form of divination

Sacred Sex and Magick, Web PATH Center
Wrap up ecstasy in love to create powerful magick, spells and healing

Spirituality without Structure, Nimue Brown
The only meaningful spiritual journey is the one you consciously undertake

The Awen Alone, Joanna van der Hoeven
An introductory guide for the solitary Druid

The Cailleach, Rachel Patterson
Goddess of the ancestors, wisdom that comes with age, the weather, time, shape-shifting and winter

The Morrigan, Morgan Daimler
On shadowed wings and in raven's call, meet the ancient Irish Goddess of war, battle, prophecy, death, sovereignty, and magic

Urban Ovate, Brendan Howlin
Simple, accessible techniques to bring Druidry to the wider public

Your Faery Magic, Halo Quin
Tap into your Natural Magic and become the Fey you are

Zen Druidry, Joanna van der Hoeven
Zen teachings and Druidry combine to create a peaceful life
path that is completely dedicated to the here and now

Shaman Pathways

Aubry's Dog, Melusine Draco
A practical and essential guide to using canine magical energies

Black Horse White Horse, Mélusine Draco
Feel the power and freedom as Black Horse, White Horse
guides you down the magical path of this most noble animal

Celtic Chakras, Elen Sentier
Tread the British native shaman's path, explore the Goddess
hidden in the ancient stories; walk the Celtic chakra spiral
labyrinth

Druid Shaman, Danu Forest
A practical guide to Celtic shamanism with exercises and
techniques as well as traditional lore for exploring the Celtic
Otherworld

Elen of the Ways, Elen Sentier
British shamanism has largely been forgotten: the reindeer
Goddess of the ancient Boreal forest is shrouded in mystery...
follow her deer-trods to rediscover her old ways

Following the Deer Trods, Elen Sentier
A practical handbook for anyone wanting to begin the old
British paths. Follows on from Elen of the Ways

Trees of the Goddess, Elen Sentier
Work with the trees of the Goddess and the old ways of Britain

Way of the Faery Shaman, Flavia Kate Peters
Your practical insight into Faeries and the elements they engage
to unlock real magic that is waiting to help you

Web of Life, Yvonne Ryves
A new approach to using ancient ways in these contemporary
and often challenging times to weave your life path

What people are saying about

Poppets and Magical Dolls

In *Pagan Portals – Poppets and Magical Dolls*, Lucya Starza has done it again! In her own inimitable style, she's taken a much needed subject and crammed so much information into 25,000 words that it sends the senses reeling. In pagan writings we find that 'poppets' are often talked about but not with any degree of positive information – and that when they are discussed it's usually in connection with cursing and ill-wishing. Here we find poppets and magical dolls are much more sympathetically dealt with and with numerous different ways of utilising them – including the much-loved Teddy-bear you were given as a child. Lucya has certainly been busy with her research ... a great book and an entertaining read.
Melusine Draco, author of *By Spellbook & Candle - Cursing, Hexing, Bottling & Binding* and the *Traditional Witchcraft series*

An excellent read – concise but comprehensive, and both practical and inspiring. It's definitely a valuable contribution to a subject that is too often over-simplified.
Joyce Froome, Museum of Witchcraft & Magic

Poppets are one of my favourite ways to work magic and in her *Poppets and Magical Dolls* book Lucya Starza has covered each and every aspect of them...and more. A fascinating read that not only covers history, types of poppets and uses for them, but everything else that you could possibly need to know to be able to work their magic. You won't be able to resist getting crafty...'
Rachel Patterson, author of several books on The Craft including *Witchcraft into the Wilds, Pagan Portals Moon Magic* and *Grimoire of a Kitchen Witch*

Pagan Portals

Poppets and Magical Dolls

Dolls for spellwork, witchcraft and
seasonal celebrations

Pagan Portals

Poppets and Magical Dolls

Dolls for spellwork, witchcraft and seasonal celebrations

Lucya Starza

Winchester, UK
Washington, USA

First published by Moon Books, 2018
Moon Books is an imprint of John Hunt Publishing Ltd., No. 3 East St., Alresford,
Hampshire SO24 9EE, UK
office1@jhpbooks.net
www.johnhuntpublishing.com
www.moon-books.net

For distributor details and how to order please visit the 'Ordering' section on our website.

ISBN: 978 1 78535 721 3
978 1 78535 722 0 (ebook)
Library of Congress Control Number: 2017955459

A CIP catalogue record for this book is available from the British Library.

Design: Stuart Davies

Printed and bound by CPI Group (UK) Ltd, Croydon, CR0 4YY, UK

We operate a distinctive and ethical publishing philosophy in
all areas of our business, from our global network of authors to
production and worldwide distribution.

Contents

I would like to thank the Museum of Witchcraft and Magic in Boscastle, Cornwall, and the Horniman Museum in South East London for their assistance in writing this book. I am also totally indebted to my husband, John Davies, for his encouragement, proofreading and patience.

Introduction

The Oldest Type of Magic

Anyone who puts a fairy on top of their Yule tree is employing doll magic – to guard their home as well as to bring enchantment into the house in the depths of winter. Although in England and America that specific tradition of tree dressing might be relatively recent, dolls, effigies and images of people, animals, spirits and deities have been used for magical purposes since very early times.

The oldest dolls discovered by archaeologists were probably not considered children's toys by the societies that made them. Models of human and animal figures were used for religious, ritual and cultural purposes by ancient people; in fact, image magic is prehistoric. Cave paintings might have been used for this, although we have no way of knowing for sure. The earliest humanoid figurine discovered is that of a lion-headed person. It is an ivory sculpture discovered in the Hohlenstein-Stadel, a German cave, in 1939. The earliest known entirely human figure is the Venus of Hohle Fels. It is an Upper Palaeolithic figurine of a woman made of mammoth ivory. Dated to between 35,000 and 40,000 years old, it is one of many early three-dimensional depictions of female forms found throughout Europe and into Siberia. It isn't known exactly what purpose such figurines served, but theories that they were used for fertility magic or represented an ancient Goddess or venerated matriarchal ancestor resonate.

By the time of the Egyptian and Mesopotamian civilisations, image magic was undeniably big business. One of the oldest spells recorded – on a Mesopotamian clay tablet from the second millennium BCE – is a healing spell that involves creating a clay effigy. It is a cure for dog-bite, according to Professor Owen

Davies in *The Oxford Illustrated History of Magic & Witchcraft*. The spell instructs you to take some clay, rub it on the wound and then use it to form a small model of the dog. Say a short incantation over the clay figure then leave it on an outside wall facing the sun to dry and crumble. As that happens, so will the wound dry up. Today, of course, I'd recommend going to A&E if you get bitten by a dog and as first aid I'd probably suggest covering the wound with a sterilised bandage rather than clay, but I do believe a little complementary magic can help the healing process and effigy spells can still be an important part of that.

The Ancient Egyptians believed that all statues, images and figures contained something of the spirit of what they represented. One example is the 'ushabti', or 'answerers', which were small figurines representing servants intended to do the bidding of important people in whose tombs they were buried.

Greek and Roman children did have dolls – although they were often more than just playthings. Young girls made clothes for their dolls and, on marrying, dedicated them to a deity; often the Greek Goddess Artemis or her Roman equivalent Diana. Magical effigies were also used in other ways in Graeco-Roman practice, according to Martin Duffy, author of *Effigy: Of Graven Image and Holy Idol*. Kolossoi were small dolls used for ritual purposes – often curses. They were named for a victim, melted or broken and then taken to a cemetery where the spirits of the restless dead would intercede on the magician's behalf to give them what they desired. This technique travelled to Britain and is possibly the origins of folk magic traditions using effigies in this country.

The title of this book includes the term 'poppet', which is a word used in traditional English magic. It comes from the Middle English 'popet', meaning a small child or doll, and since medieval times could refer to a small human figure employed in witchcraft and sorcery as well as for children's toys. According to Martin Duffy, the earliest mention of the word poppet in England is in a 10th century charter in which a widow and her son were charged and had their land confiscated for putting an iron nail in an effigy. The root of the word is the Latin 'pupa', meaning a baby girl, and is also an early form of the term 'puppet'. It is the word I was taught to use when I was training in the Craft and it is one I like. After all, a poppet is a name of endearment meaning a sweet little thing, often used for a favourite child. When I create a magical doll, it is in some ways like a little child to me, although one made of fabric, wood, clay, wax or other things than flesh and blood.

Dolls are still a commonly crafted item for use in sympathetic magic, following the idea that things that look like something have a sympathetic and symbolic connection to that thing. Created in the likeness of individuals, dolls can be used to represent them in spells to help, heal or harm. This book is about the many ways in which dolls can be used in magic – how to make them, enchant them and employ them in modern witchcraft as well as offering an overview of folk customs.

In simple terms, when casting spells, you generally either create a mental picture of what it is you want to happen and put energy into that to make it so in the real world, or you create a physical object to represent your desired effect – and a magical doll is one of the best and most time-honoured ways of doing that.

You might be wondering why I've not so far mentioned the term 'Voodoo doll'. Well, I have now – and I'll later go into more details – but I will explain here why it isn't my preferred phrase. It is a common misconception that a principal element of Voodoo (or Vodou or Hoodoo) is sticking pins into dolls as a curse; that misconception comes from 20th century books and films by white Americans and Europeans who didn't fully understand the tradition. The term 'poppet' is older and less associated with cultural appropriation, especially if used by an English witch like myself.

Another popular misconception is that poppets are only used as a focus for cursing. This is most certainly not the case. Although our ancestors were not averse to sticking pins into an effigy of someone they disliked with the intention of causing them harm, as can be seen from objects in places such as the Museum of Witchcraft and Magic in Cornwall, there are plenty of examples of poppets being used for helpful magic such as healing – including the Mesopotamian dog-bite spell.

Modern witches use poppets to help bring all sorts of benefits to their lives and to the lives of others. Whether you want to attract love, wealth or happiness, or are planning for exam success, a new job, a home move, a happy marriage, a baby or the best results from a medical procedure, poppet magic can complement your actions in the mundane world to achieve your desire. I will be talking about curses too as they are a part of traditional witchcraft, even if you personally choose never to use them.

Figurines and effigies are, of course, a huge part of many spiritual and religious practices beyond sympathetic magic. They can help us visualise Gods and Goddesses, ancestors and other beings from mythology in order to petition them or honour them in rituals and, like the Yule tree fairy, they have a role in seasonal celebrations and festivals.

Dolls are certainly not just for children. For witches, they can be our companions in magic and protectors of our homes, symbolise the God and Goddess on our altars and be practical tools for casting spells. The one thing poppets are not, are toys. Always take magical practices seriously. It is fine to try out poppet making to learn more about it, but never do it just for fun. As the saying goes: 'Be careful what you wish for...'

Chapter 1

Dolls our Mothers Gave Us

When you were a child, did you have a special doll? Perhaps it wasn't human-looking, but a Teddy bear or even a plastic gonk. Dolls and other toys can have a talismanic quality. It can feel as though having them keeps us safe, wards against our fears and worries, and attracts good luck. Sometimes it seems they have their own personality, or perhaps a little of the personality of the person who gave them to us. When we were young they might have been our friends, helpers and confidantes as well as going on adventures of the imagination with us in play. While we might grow too old to play with dolls and toys, many of us still have them and they can still be there for us if we need them.

As an adult, your old dolls or toys might have a place as ornaments in your bedroom or be stored in the attic, but it would feel wrong to throw them out. If you didn't keep any of your childhood dolls, perhaps you have one you were given as an adult by a friend or loved one. Maybe it has sentimental value or cheers you up and reminds you of the giver. Perhaps it acts as a lucky charm.

Personally, I have several dolls and other toys from my childhood and a few given to me over the years. I also have a Kipling rucksack, which comes with the brand's iconic monkey. There have been times when I was travelling somewhere or to something I was nervous about and have looked at that irrepressible-looking monkey and wished for luck.

The Slavic fairy story Vasilisa the Beautiful tells of a young woman who gains help from a magical doll given to her by her mother. It comes from *Russian Fairy Tales* by Alexander Afanasyev and is worth reading in full, but here is a short version:

On her deathbed, Vasilisa's mother gave her a small wooden doll and told her the doll was very special. If she was ever in need, she should give the doll a little food and water and ask for help. Vasilisa's father remarried but, as is often the case in fairy tales, the stepmother was not only cruel, but had two daughters of her own who treated Vasilisa badly. They set her the most difficult and unpleasant household chores, which she nevertheless accomplished perfectly – with the magical help of her doll.

The father was a merchant and his work often took him travelling. On one occasion, when he had been away for a long time, Vasilisa's stepmother sold the family home and moved the girls to a gloomy hut at the edge of a forest. Their nearest neighbour was the feared hag Baba Yaga, who it was said was in the habit of eating unwelcome visitors.

One winter's day, Vasilisa's stepmother put out the fire in the hut, leaving only a single candle alight to work by as the sun set. The stepsisters, who were in a particularly mean mood, blew out the candle and told Vasilisa she would be blamed. The only solution, they said, was for Vasilisa to go to their neighbour, Baba Yaga, and beg for a light.

Obviously, this wasn't something anyone would want to do, but without fire the family would perish, so the next morning Vasilisa set off through the wood, taking her doll with her.

After a long walk, during which time she was passed by three unusual riders – one in white, one in red and one in black – Vasilisa came to a house that stood on chicken legs, walled by a fence of human bones topped by skulls with glowing eye-sockets. It was the home of Baba Yaga. As she watched, the three riders again passed her, riding through the hag's house.

Vasilisa was terrified, but nevertheless approached the strange dwelling, knocked on the door and asked for fire. She thought herself lucky the hag didn't eat her at once. Instead, Baba Yaga said she must work to earn the flame. If she failed, she would kill her. Not only was Vasilisa expected to clean the house, wash clothes and cook, she was also instructed to separate rotten grain from good grain and poppy seeds from soil.

The normal chores she did over the course of a day – although she was again surprised to see the three riders enter and leave the house. The other tasks were, of course, impossible for one girl to do unaided in the time allotted. Terrified she would be eaten, Vasilisa's only hope was to secretly ask her little doll for help, and it did. The doll told Vasilisa to sleep. When she awoke the tasks were completed perfectly – although Vasilisa was surprised to then see three disembodied hands squeeze oil from the seeds.

Baba Yaga could complain of nothing – although she looked as though she wanted to. Instead, she asked if the young woman had any questions.

Vasilisa asked who or what the riders were, and was told the white one was day, the red one the sun and the black one was night. She thought, then, of asking about the disembodied hands, but the doll quivered a warning in her pocket and Vasilisa realised she should not ask more. In return, Baba Yaga asked Vasilisa how she had succeeded in the tasks. Wisely not wishing to give away the precise nature of her magical doll, Vasilisa simply said: 'By my mother's blessing.'

Baba Yaga fell into a rage and said she wanted nobody with any kind of blessing in her house. She threw Vasilisa out, but kept her side of the bargain and gave her a skull full of burning coals.

Returning to her stepmother's hut, Vasilisa found that no one had been able to light any candles or fire from the time she left until the moment she returned with coals. But, once the fires were lit, the glowing skull grew brighter and hotter.

Fire spread through the house, burning the stepmother and stepsisters to ashes, although Vasilisa escaped. She buried the skull so no one would be harmed by it again, left the ruined hut and made her way to the city.

Once there – again with the help and advice of her magical doll – she became famous as the most skilled weaver in the land, married the Tsar and eventually found her long-lost father. As in many fairy tales, they all lived happily ever after.

I'm not suggesting the dolls we hold onto as adults in the real world are *quite* as magical as that, but I do believe they can act as lucky charms. The well-wishing of the giver imbues them with the power to give us strength when we need to face our fears or have difficult decisions to make. They aren't going to sift poppy seeds while you sleep, but asking your doll for help before you go to bed might prompt guiding dreams, lead you to wake the next morning with the answer to a problem in your thoughts or give you the confidence to do what must be done.

Practical Magic: Find Your Helper Doll

If you still have a doll, bear or other toy from when you were a child, find it. If not, dig out any doll or toy given to you that has sentimental value. If you don't have anything that fits the bill, treat yourself to one as a gift to yourself. It doesn't matter if it is small – even on a key ring – it is the way you feel about the doll that counts.

- Sit in a quiet place alone with your doll and study it carefully.
- Examine how you feel about it and what memories it brings up.
- Does your doll have a name?
- Ask your doll if it will help you.
- Wait silently and see if you can sense an answer.

- If that answer is yes, thank your doll.
- Make it an offering of a little food and drink, by putting them in front of the doll. A little tea and a shared biscuit would be fine. (Spent offerings should be put outdoors afterwards.)
- Put your doll where you will see it. If it is small, you could carry it in a pocket or bag.
- When you are in need, ask your doll for help.

Chapter 2

An Easy Way to Make and Use Poppets

A poppet, as explained earlier, is a traditional name for a doll used to represent an individual in spellcasting. Sometimes a poppet is created because the person in question isn't there when the spell is being cast. It works on the principles of imitation, or sympathetic, magic – operating on the idea that something that looks like an individual can take their place in magical acts. You can also make poppets of people who are present – including yourself – because they are great to use as a focus. In fact, making poppets to represent yourself – or an aspect of yourself that you want to boost or aid – is the main way I would recommend starting out.

Poppets don't have to look realistic – they can be highly stylised. Obviously if you are skilled at sewing, knitting, carving, modelling, drawing and so on you can use your talents for good effect, but even if you have no artistic skills and are rubbish at making things, you can still quickly make a simple and effective poppet.

How to Make a Simple Poppet

Gather together the following items:

For the body
A clean cotton handkerchief once owned by the person the spell is for or a square of fabric from one of their old garments

Stuffing
A few strands of their hair (get this from a comb or hairbrush; you don't have to cut it from anyone's head)
More small bits of cloth from their garment, or cotton wool, if

you don't have enough hair to stuff the doll

Other things
Wool or string
Scissors
A marker pen

Place the hair, cloth bits or a cotton wool ball in the centre of the handkerchief or square of fabric. This will form the head. Bunch the fabric over the stuffing and tie the wool or string around it to form a neck, leaving either end of the wool to be the poppet's arms.

Trim the wool or string to a suitable length. The rest of the handkerchief, under the head and arms, represents a loose body or clothing.

Write the person's name on the edge of the fabric. You can draw on any features that are relevant for the spell – although these can be simple shapes, dots or lines. Eyes can be represented by tiny crosses or circles.

Then say three times: '*I name you XXX.*'

Your poppet is now ready for you to cast your spell on.

Practical Magic: A Simple Poppet and Candle Spell

This simple spell can be used when you want to send magical wishes to someone, including yourself. Perhaps you want to sending healing energy, wish good luck in an exam or test; boost success in a job interview, new venture or contest; wish travellers a safe journey; cheer someone up if they are feeling down or make sure any activity goes as well as it can.

You need
A poppet to represent the person for whom the spell is intended
A tea light candle and tea light holder
Matches

Pop the tea light candle out of its case and, with the end of a match, inscribe one word on the candle to represent what the spell is for. Examples could include: *health, good luck, success, safe journey, happiness* or just *blessings.* Put the candle back in its case and then put that in the tea light holder. Place it in front of the poppet and light the candle while saying a few words about what you wish for. It could be as simple as: '*XXX, may you have good luck in what you are doing at this time.*'

Let the candle burn so its light falls on the poppet (obviously be careful not to place the doll so close you set fire to it!).

Moving Forward

While there is nothing wrong with that basic poppet spell, you can make your magic more effective by how you make the doll, what you put inside it and what you dress it with. By deliberately using the magical properties of materials, colours, herbs and other components, you can specifically tailor your poppet for its purpose. The next chapters will show various ways of making poppets and enchanting them.

Chapter 3

The Body of the Matter

Poppets can be made from all sorts of materials: cloth, wool, wax, wood, clay, carved roots, woven straw, corn shafts, fruit or vegetables and paper are all traditional. You don't have to stay traditional though, you can make them from Plasticine, you can upcycle packaging material – you could even make a 3D print-out of plastic if you wanted to. I'm all for moving with the times.

Some modern poppets are repurposed from mass-produced toys and dolls – and you can even buy 'Voodoo doll' kits, but I don't think they work as effectively as something you have made yourself and there are two good reasons why. Firstly, the poppet should have a connection to the person the spell is for and you can use things associated with them to make, stuff or adorn the poppet. Secondly, you start to imbue the doll with purpose as you make it – your thoughts, feelings and intentions go into every act you perform while putting the doll together. There's a reason witchcraft is known as 'the craft'.

Generally I make small poppets, between 5cm-10cm in length. You need less material to make and stuff a small poppet than a big one plus they are easier to store, carry around or hide (if you need your magic to be discreet). Don't feel you always have to do that though – you can make your dolls as large as you like.

Fabric

In modern witchcraft, poppets are often simple sewn dolls made from two gingerbread-person shapes cut out of fabric then stitched together around the edges. You can draw a basic pattern yourself on a piece of paper. This is easily done by folding a piece of paper in half down the middle, drawing one side of the doll against the fold and cutting it out so that when you open it up you have two symmetrical halves joined in the middle. Practise until you get a shape you are pleased with. Put that paper pattern onto a double layer of fabric, pin it in place through both layers, then cut out both sides of the doll at the same time.

If you prefer to use a pattern someone else has designed, they are easy to find in books on doll-making, online or in craft shops – or you could draw around a gingerbread person dough cutter.

For material, you can upcycle an old garment worn by the person the poppet will represent to give it personal connection, or use new fabric in a natural colour or one that ties in with the purpose of the spell (there's more on colour symbolism later in this chapter). Natural ingredients are best for any type of spellwork, but if the only old garment you can find to reuse is a tatty pair of nylon knickers, go ahead and use them. The connection to the individual is the most important thing.

If you are using new fabric, felt is easy to cut and sew, and doesn't fray. No need to hem – a simple running stitching by hand around the edges is all you need to hold it together. However, overstitch or blanket stitch are more durable on fabrics that fray and will do a better job of keeping loose bits inside. Stuff the doll as you go, filling it a little at a time and making sure all you want inside is there before doing the final few stitches. If you prefer very neat edges, sew a seam by putting the right sides of the cut-out doll pieces facing each other and stitching a centimetre around most of the edge, then turn the doll the right way round, stuff it and overstitch the rest closed.

Features can be drawn, sewn or stuck on afterwards. Simple crosses or circles for eyes and a line for a mouth are okay, but you can add other stylised features if you like. You can use beads, buttons or bought sets of dolls' eyes.

Wool

If you can knit or crochet, you can bind your spell in every stitch. Use the small poppet knitting pattern below or source a pattern for a knitted doll online or from a hobby shop. Choose pure wool as a preference, but you can reuse wool unravelled from garments worn by the person the poppet represents, which might not always be 100 per cent natural. You can also cut up old knitted garments for a sewn poppet in the same way as a fabric doll, but you will need to bind the edges with blanket stitch to stop it unravelling.

When you make a knitted doll as part of a spell, you can create a chant or mantra to say in your head over and over as you work. Something like: '*In and round and out I cast, this spell I do weave to last.*' However, if you are a novice knitter, just concentrating on following the pattern is fine too.

Small Poppet Knitting Pattern

With this simple knitting pattern for a small poppet you knit the body all in one go, starting at one leg, then the other leg, then joining them together and knitting the body and head. The arms are knitted separately and sewn on. Use 4mm needles and double knit wool. You can use three cotton wool balls for stuffing, or a similar quantity of other material such as small pieces of fabric. Put hair, herbs and so on inside the middle of the cotton wool balls to keep them in place.

Legs and body
Cast on 7 stitches. Knit 6 rows of stocking stitch then cut the wool and tie off the end, leaving a longish thread. Push the first leg to the back of your needle then cast on another 7 stitches. Knit 6 rows of stocking stitch again, then knit right across both legs – 14 stitches in total – for 14 rows in stocking stitch. Decrease by knitting twice into each stitch so you have 7 stitches, then cut off a longish amount of wool, thread it through the 7 stitches and pull them tight to form the top of the head and tie off the thread.

Arms
Cast on 6 stitches, knit 5 rows of stocking stitch, then cast off.
Repeat for the second arm.

Sewing, stuffing and finishing
Using the thread from the top of the head, sew up the back of the
head and body to the top of the legs and fasten off the wool. Put
two cotton wool balls (or other stuffing) into the body cavity.
Poke any herbs, crystals or other items inside the middle of the
cotton wool balls. Cut the third cotton wool ball in half and put
half into the fold of each leg. Stitch between the crotch, then
down and around the bottom of each leg. Loosely stitch around
the doll between the two cotton wool balls, then pull the ends of
the wool to gather in the stitches to form a neck, fastening them
off.

Fold the arms in half and stitch along the seam, then stitch
each arm to the body. No need to stuff the arms.

Poke the loose ends of wool into the doll's body for neatness.
Embroider eyes and any other features onto the doll afterwards.

Knotted Poppet from Wool or Cloth

If you really can't sew or knit, you can tie cloth or lengths of
wool into a doll shape in an advanced form of the simple poppet
described in chapter 2. Below is how to make knotted wool or
string poppets – sometimes called yarn dolls.

You need
Cardboard
Wool or string
Scissors

Cut an oblong of stiff cardboard the same height as you want
your poppet to be. Loop the wool or string around the cardboard.
You will need about 50 loops for a small doll.

Slide a piece of wool between the loops and the cardboard and push it up to the top, then tie it in a tight knot to mark the top of the head. Slide the wool loops off the cardboard, then tie a length of wool in a tight knot around the neck. Pull a few loops sideways to form the arms. Tie a strand tightly around the middle of the poppet to form a waist and others where you want the wrists. Cut the loops to form hands. You can leave the bottom of the doll as a skirt or you can separate the loops into legs and tie at the ankles. Finally trim loose ends.

Clay and Dough

There is something satisfying about moulding a poppet into shape with your own hands. Clay is one of the oldest ways in which magical dolls were created. It isn't difficult. Take some clay, mould it into an oval shape, pinch a neck and form the head into a suitable shape. With a knife, cut the bottom of the oval to form legs, then cut slits at the side of the body to form arms. Pinch and shape the body, head, legs and arms until your poppet looks like a person. Use a pin, knife tip or modelling tools to craft finer features. The wonderful thing about clay is that if it doesn't look right you can squish it down and start again – at least until it dries. It doesn't have to be realistic. My own efforts nearly always look something like Morph – the little animated figure from the 1970s BBC children's programme – but it doesn't matter. A stylised result is fine. Having said that, it can help you visualise the poppet as the person it is supposed to be if you add distinguishing marks – general body shape, for example.

These days there are many different types of clay available, from natural soil dug from the earth to man-made PVC-based polymers such as Fimo. In general, it is best to use natural materials when doing magic – and moulding your doll from the body of Mother Earth has obvious symbolic resonance. If you dig it from the ground yourself, even better, but most of us modern witches do not live by riverbanks with natural clay deposits and have to make do with shop stuff. That's okay. What I would say is that if you are intending to leave the poppet outside – either as part of the spell or to dispose of the remains – make sure the material you use is biodegradable and non-toxic. Weigh up the pros and cons of what's available, easy to use and suitable for your purpose. For example, polymer clays come in a huge variety of colours – great if you are using colour correspondences or want to replicate skin tones. They are easy to model and easy to cure in an oven to set solid. Cured polymer clay is durable, but can be drilled or have nails banged in without breaking.

Salt dough is another easy-to-make option. Mix two parts plain flour with one part salt in a bowl. Very slowly mix in water until it is a doughy consistency. Turn it onto a flat surface and knead it thoroughly. Leave it to stand for 20 minutes or so before hand-moulding it or, alternatively, roll it out to a suitable thickness and use a gingerbread person cutter. Salt dough takes several days to air dry or can be dried in an oven at a very low heat – or put on top of a warm radiator. Although salt dough is natural, do be aware that salt can kill plants and is toxic to some animals, so it is best not left anywhere it might cause harm. Do think about the ingredients you want to use. For a healing spell you might choose wholemeal flour and water from a holy spring, for a love or beauty charm you might collect dew from the garden on May Day morning.

If you are too short of time to carefully source everything, you can raid the children's room for poppet-making materials. Play-Doh is a form of salt dough to which mineral oils have been added. Plasticine – which the above-mentioned Morph was moulded from – is made from calcium salts, petroleum jelly and aliphatic acids. It is easy to mould and comes in many colours, but can't be permanently set – which is good or bad depending on your spell intentions.

Whether you choose real clay, polymer clay, Plasticine or salt dough will depend on what you have available, what you prefer working with, what you intend to use the poppet for and how durable it needs to be. Unfired natural clay and dough will soften and break down in water – or if you leave them out in the rain. Wax, Plasticine and some polymer clays can be repeatedly remodelled. Herbs can be kneaded in, or you can make a cavity to put things in afterwards. Some clays will fracture or break if you try to push things like pins into them after they have dried. Plan ahead and pick your material to suit your intent.

Wax

Wax is also a traditional material for image magic. Beeswax can be made malleable just with the warmth of your hands and makes delightful poppets. It is pure and natural and frankly my favourite wax to use for poppet-making. While moulding beeswax is easy with your hands, softening ordinary hard candle wax and keeping it at the right temperature to hand-mould is difficult. Soften hard wax in a very gentle heat – use a hairdryer or put it near a radiator or in a sunny window. Put olive oil on your hands to stop the wax sticking to you and be careful not to burn yourself. Melted paraffin wax can be poured into person-shaped candle moulds or biscuit moulds and left to set. To completely melt hard wax, use a double burner or put it in a bowl that's standing in another bowl of hot water. Alternatively, place a gingerbread cutter onto oven-proof paper and drip melted wax from a lit candle into that to slowly build up a wax poppet. Craft shops also sell wax that is mouldable at hand temperature, usually for children to make candles from, but it can be used for poppet-making. Another method is to carve a figure from a lump of wax or a candle.

Be reasonably careful with it after you have made it. A wax poppet will, of course, melt if heated – which might or might not be what you want. Wax is fragile, but can also be altered reasonably easily – for example, by carving it – as part of your spell.

Wood

You don't have to be skilled at woodcarving to make wooden magical dolls. The easiest way is to use a wooden spoon or fork. A cooking spoon makes a large doll, but a wooden teaspoon or fork of the disposable type often found in street food markets makes a great small doll. Draw or paint a face on the round bit and let the handle form the body. You can make arms with pipe cleaners or stick on small lengths of wood (wooden stirrers or lolly sticks, for example). Make simple clothes using fabric – an oblong with a small hole cut in the middle for the neck, tied around the waist. If the arms aren't flexible, you will need to put the clothing on from the bottom before attaching the arms. With forks, you can cut down the tines to look like short hair. The tines can also be used to help hold folded lengths of wool in place for long hair, although you will also need glue. Trim the tines after the wool is fixed. Wooden spoons are often made of beech, which magically symbolises luck and success.

Peg dolls are another easy option. In Victorian times, clothes pegs were a single piece of wood, usually willow, with a shaped split down the middle and a rounded top. So many children made dolls out of them that they got the nickname dolly pegs. You can still buy dolly pegs and they are great as poppets. Draw or paint features on the head, then glue and twist wire or a pipe cleaner in place for arms. Make clothes if you want to. Magically, willow is associated with love, protection and healing.

If you prefer to make poppets from wood in its more natural state, you could go on a forest walk and look for a fallen twig with the right shape for a figure. As you walk, ask the spirits of the forest to guide you to what you are looking for and to help you in your magical endeavour. Use a craft knife to trim twigs and remove the bark, then carve or draw features.

Roots and Fruits

Pretty much everyone, witch or not, has heard of the mandrake root being the perfect ingredient for creating a homunculus. Homunculi are more magical creatures than dolls, but roots that naturally look a bit like a person can be used for making poppets. I wouldn't recommend mandrake roots for beginners though as they are hard to grow and poisonous, even if they don't scream so loud they kill anyone who is listening when they are pulled from the ground, despite what folklore says. As an alternative to mandrake, white bryony roots were traditionally used for male dolls and black bryony for female. There are plenty of other roots you can use. If you are a gardener, keep a look out for likely specimens next time you are weeding. I've pulled docks with highly suggestive nether parts in my time.

You can also easily carve a potato into a face or stick things to it for features and feet. Like mandrake and various other magical plants, potatoes are in the *Solanaceae* family, so have some of the same magical properties without being dangerous. In a similar way you can use hard fruit such as apples and pears, while pumpkins and gourds can be carved into faces for more than just Halloween lanterns. Fruit, veg and roots will rot unless they are carefully preserved, but the fact that they are completely biodegradable makes them ideal for some spellwork.

Corn, Straw, Reeds and Raffia

These make very traditional-looking folk art dolls and straw or reeds are particularly used in Ireland for Brigid dolls at Candlemas or Imbolc (see chapter 12).

If you are using corn, reeds or straw, soak a bundle in water so the strands become pliable. Raffia tends to be naturally softer. Take a bunch of strands and tie string or cotton a couple of centimetres from one end, then fold the long ends over the tied section to form a neat head. Tie more string or cotton around the straw where the neck would be. Take a few straws and push them through the doll to form the arms, then tie string or cotton underneath the arms to hold them in place and to help the remaining straws splay out to look like a skirt. Form the hands by tying where the wrists would be, then trim the straws to the length you desire. You can weave in dried flowers as you make the doll or afterwards and then dress the doll with fabric for clothing.

Pipe Cleaner or Wire Poppets

Remember making stick figures out of pipe cleaners when you were young? Well, you can use the same technique as the basis for easy poppets. For the basic method, make a loop near one end of the pipe cleaner as a head, leaving a little for an arm at one side. For the other arm, fold the long part of the pipe cleaner in on itself, the same length as the first arm. Fold the pipe cleaner around the neck and down for the body, then fold two legs in a similar way to the arms. You can do the same thing with other types of wire for varying stiffness.

Wrap wool or strips of fabric around the wire poppet if you want. I like to make the heads more of a feature by taking a cotton wool ball and inserting it in the wire loop, then wrapping plenty of wool around it. I sometimes pop appropriate herbs, crystals or personal items inside the cotton wool ball first. Afterwards, sew or stick on eyes or other features. You can make little clothes to put on the wrapped wire skeleton, tying or sticking them in place. The great thing about wire dolls is that they are flexible, but reasonably strong.

Paper and Cardboard

The Victorians loved cardboard cut-outs you could dress up with paper clothing using flaps at the edges to fold over the shoulders or waist. You can use the same thing for spellwork and they are easy to make. Draw an outline of a figure on cardboard, cut it out and paint or draw features as you desire. Then draw clothes on paper and cut them out, leaving flaps at the edges to fold around the doll. The clothes should add to the spell's purpose

– wedding dresses, scholars' gowns, business suits or witches' cloaks and hats all have different symbolism. They don't have to be works of art – simple and stylised is fine. If you are non-artistic you can buy cardboard doll shapes from hobby shops then copy pictures of clothing from magazines or photos. You can easily write your wishes onto the body of the doll too.

You can also make papier-mâché dolls. Make a doll-shaped frame from fine wire mesh, then cover this with strips of paper and wallpaper paste. Leave it to dry, then paint the doll as you desire. Paper can even be used in the same way as fabric poppets – cut out two identical simple doll shapes from paper, sandwich any stuffing material between them, then glue or staple them together around the edges. Paper dolls might not be as durable as other kinds, but are fine for quick spells using easy to find materials. If you are intending to bury, burn or expose the doll to the elements, paper is quickly biodegradable.

Corks

Champagne or similar sparkling wine corks are the best type to upcycle into a doll as the rounded top forms the head. First you can paint the cork. When that's dry, add features with marker pens or paint. Get some slightly stretchy fabric – ideally from something worn by the person the poppet is to represent. Old socks and t-shirts are good. Cut out an oval of fabric at least twice as long as the cork to form loose clothing, then cut a hole slightly smaller than the neck of the cork. Push that over the doll. For arms, loop wire or a pipe cleaner round the doll, under the clothing. Twist the ends of the wire through the loop a few times until the ends are at the sides of the doll. Trim as desired or loop the ends back to make hands. If you want legs, cut another cork in two lengthwise (you will need a strong, sharp craft knife for this), trim as necessary and stick to the bottom of the body with glue.

Edible Dolls

According to folklorist Edward Lovett, edible dolls representing famous people were a traditional custom all over Europe in the past. They were often buns or gingerbread. An example he gave in *Handbook to the Exhibition of the Lovett Collection of Dolls 1914* was gingerbread models of Wellington sold at fairs in England in the 1850s. Eating the gingerbread was considered a way of taking in the noble qualities of the person. You could make a gingerbread person in the shape of a superhero or other heroic archetype and eat it to imbue yourself with those qualities. There is a recipe for one type of gingerbread doll in chapter 8.

The Colours of Magic

Colour is a hugely important part of spellcraft; you can make any magic more effective using the symbolism or correspondences associated with colour. For poppet making, fabrics, wax and modelling materials come in a huge variety of colours these days, but whether you pick a specific coloured material to make your poppet out of, paint colour on afterwards or use coloured fabrics, threads or other accessories to dress up your doll, you can boost its intended purpose using colour correspondences. You can pick one because of what it means to you personally or you can use the associations ascribed to colours in various magical traditions. Either way is fine so long as you feel comfortable with the result.

Here are some of the colours associated with the elements, which you could use to infuse your doll with appropriate attributes:

Earth: Brown, black or ochre. Represents stability, strength, the physical world, our bodies and groundedness.
Air: Pale blue, white, pale yellow. Represents thoughts, intellect, communication, our breath.

Fire: Red, orange, bright yellow. Represents passion, action, our spirit.

Water: Blue, green. Represents emotions, our souls, our blood, the tides of change.

Planetary correspondences are also associated with specific colours in the western esoteric magical tradition, which is one system commonly used by witches. Here are the planetary colours and meanings:

Moon: Blue, white or silver. Represents women's mysteries, illusion, glamour, sleep, peace, beauty, prophecy, dreams, emotions, travel, fertility, women's health, insight, wisdom.

Mars: Red. Represents battles, courage, victory, success, strength, conviction, rebellion, defence, wards, protection, anything military.

Mercury: Orange. Represents communication, the arts, writing, transport, change, luck, gambling, fortune, chance, creativity, making deals, trickery, crimes (solving them), work issues needing discussion.

Jupiter: Purple or dark blue. Represents abundance, protection, prosperity, strength, health, wealth, management roles.

Venus: Green or pink. Represents love, birth, fertility, romance, gentleness, pregnancy, friendship, passion happiness.

Saturn: Black. Represents banishing, protection, wisdom, spirituality, cleansing, astral magic, weeding the garden, honouring or remembering the dead.

Sun: Yellow/gold. Represents success, fame, wealth, health, prosperity, promotion, getting a new job

Stuffing and Filling

Although I've mentioned stuffing poppets already, I'll go into more details here because if your doll is to be used for a magical purpose there are three important aspects to what you put inside:

- Filler to pad out soft dolls.
- Components that physically link the doll to the person represented.
- Things that relate or correspond to the desired magical outcome.

Neutral fillers

This is really only needed for soft dolls, such as those made from fabric or wool, rather than for solid or hard dolls. It is just to give some shape. Ideally, use as little neutral filler as possible. To pack your poppet with power, just use components that physically link the doll to whoever it represents or things that correspond to your spell. However, sometimes you don't have sufficient of those things and you don't want your doll to go half-stuffed.

If that's the case, try to use clean, natural fillers. Some New Orleans Voodoo doll makers suggest using Spanish moss. This plant material is native to central and South America, where it was widely used as packing. It isn't traditionally used for stuffing poppets in English magic – straw, wool or horsehair would have more historical authenticity. For small poppets, I often use pure cotton wool as a natural, neutral filler. Being a city witch rather than a country witch, it is easier for me to pop out to the shops and buy it than it is to pop out to a barn to get straw.

Physical links

The more connection a poppet has with the person in question the better, so stuffing it with their old socks is perfect – although you will probably need to cut them up into tiny pieces first. Ideally, also put a few strands of their hair or nail clippings inside. Witches sometimes call these types of things taglocks – a term that traditionally means a matted knot of hair. If you have a long time to plan your doll's creation, save up the hair that collects in a hairbrush and use that as the main filler. If you are making a dough, wax or clay doll then you can chop hairs up fine and knead them into the modelling material before starting to shape it.

Packing in correspondences
The third type of filler relates or corresponds to the desired magical outcome. This can be dried herbs, flowers or leaves that have the appropriate magical association. Herbal magic is a very wide subject, but one book I would recommend is *A Kitchen Witch's World of Magical Herbs and Plants* by Rachel Patterson, which is a constant source of reference for me. The list below offers some suggestions, but do be aware that some of the herbs and plants mentioned are poisonous.

Banishment and Exorcism: Angelica, basil, bergamot, birch, blackthorn, clove, clover, cumin, horseradish, juniper, mint, mugwort, nettle, peony, rosemary, sage, Solomon's seal, thistle, yarrow, wormwood.

Bindings: Ivy, honeysuckle.

Cleansing and Purifying: Bay, birch, broom, cedar, hawthorn, lavender, mint, mugwort, parsley, pine, sage, tansy, thyme, willow, wormwood.

Confidence and Courage: Birch, carnation, fennel, ginger, thyme, yarrow.

Curses: Blackthorn, elder.

Dreams: Ash, catnip, chamomile, heather, jasmine, lavender mugwort, poppy, rose, star anise, yarrow.

Divination: Angelica, beech, blackthorn, hazel, rowan, Saint John's wort, witch hazel, wormwood, yarrow.

Escape and Breaking Free: Buddleia, celandine.

Fertility: Birch, cornflower, geranium, hawthorn, hazel, oak, parsley, pine, poppy, sunflower, walnut.

Fidelity: Ivy, honeysuckle, magnolia, nutmeg.

Happiness: Basil, borage, catnip, celandine, crocus, cyclamen, daisy, hawthorn, hyacinth, lavender, lily of the valley, marigold, marjoram, meadowsweet, parsley, peony, Saint John's wort, sunflower, sweet pea, yarrow.

Healing and Health: Angelica, ash, bay, burdock, calamus, cinnamon, coltsfoot, comfrey, coriander, cowslip, dock, echinacea, elder, eucalyptus, fennel, feverfew, flax, garlic, hazel, horehound, hyssop, juniper, lemon balm, lungwort, mallow, marjoram, mint, mistletoe, mugwort, nettle, oak, pine, plantain, rose, rosemary, rowan, rue, sage, Saint John's wort, sorrel, tansy, thyme, vervain, willow.

Legal Matters: Calendula, celandine.

Improving One's Mood: Geranium, lemon balm, St John's wort, valerian.

Love: Aster, basil, birch, bleeding heart, caraway, cardamom, catnip, chamomile, chestnut, cinnamon, cinquefoil, clove, clover, coltsfoot, cumin, cyclamen, daisy, dittany of Crete, dock, elm, geranium, ginger, hawthorn, hazel, heather, hyacinth, iris, ivy, jasmine, juniper, lady's mantle, lavender, lemon balm, lilac, lovage, mallow, mandrake, marjoram, meadowsweet, mistletoe, myrtle, orchid, pansy, passion flower, periwinkle, poppy, primrose, rose, rosemary, rowan, Saint John's wort, sandalwood, sea holly, sorrel, thyme, tulip, willow, yarrow.

Luck: Angelica, beech, broom, clover, elm, hazel, heather, holly, marigold, nutmeg, oak, peony, poppy, rose, star anise, sunflower.

Memory and Mental Powers: Rosemary, sage, lemon balm.

Mourning the Dead/Rebirth: Cypress, elder, yew.

New Ventures and New Beginnings: Birch.

Protection: Angelica, ash, basil, bay, benzoin, birch, blackthorn, bracken, broom, cactus, cedar, clove, clover, comfrey, dill, elder, fennel, feverfew, garlic, geranium, ginger, gorse, hawthorn, hazel, heather, holly, honeysuckle, juniper, lavender, mandrake, marigold, marjoram, mint, mistletoe, mugwort, mustard, myrrh, nettle, nutmeg, oak, parsley, pine, plantain, rose, rosemary, rowan, rue, sage, Saint John's wort, self heal, Solomon's seal, star anise, sunflower, tansy, thistle, valerian, vervain, violet, willow, witch hazel, wormwood, yarrow.

Sleeping in Peace: Hops, lavender, rosemary, thyme, valerian, vervain.

Success: Beech, cinnamon, clover, ginger, rowan, sage, Solomon's seal, sunflower.

Wealth and Abundance: Basil, chamomile, clove, clover, coriander, cumin, dandelion, ginger, honesty, mint, oak, rose, sage.

If the spell is intended to affect a specific body part – to heal an injury, for example – you might want to make that bit of the poppet as realistic as possible. Representations of internal organs can be fashioned out of felt, wool, wax or card and inserted into stuffed dolls or dolls with hollow frames before they are completed, or attached to the outside if that isn't possible. This doesn't only have to be done for healing spells. There are historic examples of poppets used for love magic with hearts sewn in. You can also write words or symbols onto slips of paper to put inside.

If you have made a wax, dough or clay doll, you can cut a slit into the body before it has hardened, insert a small item, then smooth it over. You can also hollow out cavities in dolls, including those made from carved wood, roots, vegetables or corks, to stuff with herbs or other things. If necessary use a little clay or wax to seal them inside. Bags of herbs and other materials can be added to dolls' under clothing if the body is unsuitable for stuffing. There's more on this in the next chapter.

Practical Crafting: Make a Doll

The dolls described here are designed to be easy to make, but it is a good idea to practise the basic skills of crafting dolls before doing so as part of a spell. Although you imbue dolls with correspondences and connections as you make them, they are not finished magical dolls unless you fully enchant them. So, it doesn't matter if you make mistakes with your early efforts. Try one or two techniques described in this chapter and find out which method of doll making feels most natural to you.

Chapter 4

Finishes and Flourishes

While the last chapter covered making dolls and what to put inside them, this is about ways to adorn, embellish and add other extras.

External Features

If you are good at drawing, painting or embroidery, you can use your skills to make your poppet look as lifelike as possible, or you could stick a photo of a person's face to a doll. But, as I've said before, most poppets are pretty stylised and that's fine. Some rudimentary external features are a good idea, especially eyes, as they are the window to the soul. How you display them can be important. If you are doing a spell to help someone clearly see the solution to a problem, you could make the eyes look wide open, but you might prefer them to look closed if it is a spell to help you sleep.

You can add other features to boost your desired effect. If you are trying to communicate with someone using a magical doll to represent them, give the poppet a mouth and ears too. For a love spell, you might draw, paint or attach a heart shape to the chest. For healing spells – and some others – representations of internal organs can be fashioned out of fabric, wool, wax, clay or card and inserted into stuffed dolls, but they can also be attached to the outside or drawn on.

Dressing up Dolly

Dress your doll in a way appropriate for the purpose of the spell. Again, this doesn't have to be realistic – a small strip or square of fabric can represent clothing, but pick a fabric that carries the right message. Use white lace for a spell for a happy wedding, a piece of business suit material for interview success, red silk for love magic, for example. You can add accessories – hats, scarves or jewellery – for added emphasis and style. Consider the meaning of jewellery. Rings can be for engagement, marriage or fidelity and individual gems will have their own significance. Common ones are amber or jet for all things witchy, citrine for wealth, rose quartz for romance, amethyst for cleansing and protection, carnelian for confidence and moonstone to boost your psychic powers. Clear quartz is the best general-purpose crystal for boosting spellwork and for healing.

Colours

Whatever colour you used for the body of your doll, more colour symbolism can be added afterwards as clothing, accessories and other adornments. You can attach ribbons, beads, buttons and strips of fabric, or paint on colourful designs. One of my friends fashioned a wonderful poppet representing a Morris dancer, to help them heal their ankle well enough to dance again. They attached tatters of wool in the colours used by their Morris side and the doll looked superb as well as feeling very magical.

Words

You can write or embroider words onto your doll. This could be its name, or you could write out your intention. If you do that, keep it simple and sum it up in one or two words if possible: *love, health, happiness, abundance, justice, career* etc. Another way you can distil the essence of words into a symbol is to create a sigil. From your word or phrase, remove all the vowels and reduce duplicate letters to a single one. Use the letters you have left to form a graphic by, for example, placing all the straight lines and curving lines on top of each other. Then draw or embroider the resulting sigil on your poppet.

Numbers

Numbers can also have personal meanings. You could add house numbers for a spell for a safe move or to protect your home, the score you want to achieve in a test, the age of the person represented and so on. You don't have to use the numeral itself – you could stitch on that amount of beads or buttons. You can also use the more mystical associations of numbers.

Zero: A circle, with all the symbolism that holds. Zero represents eternity and the state of being before creation. It is also the shape of the magical circle of protection cast by witches before spellwork or ritual.

1: The beginning, the start of a journey, being on one's own and individuality. It also represents the creative force.

2: Complementary or opposing dualities or polarity. Two represents a pair and balance, but can also symbolise conflict.

3: Three is a magical and spiritual number in many magical traditions and religions. Think mind, body and soul; the Triple Goddess; past, present and future.

4: The sides of a square; the four elements, earth, fire, water and air; the cardinal points of the compass; the four seasons.

5: The points of the pentacle and the number that represents human beings – arms, legs and head. Five can represent good fortune, but with an element of risk.

6: This represents balance, love, health and good luck.

7: Another lucky number, it is also associated with mystery and the occult. There are said to be seven heavens, seven ruling planets, seven chakras and seven wonders of the world. It also represents every day of the week.

8: The shape of number 8 is also the symbol for eternity. It represents stability and symmetry and is the number of festivals in the pagan wheel of the year and the spokes of the Buddhist wheel for the eight-fold path to enlightenment.

9: This is another sacred and magical number, representing 3x3.

10: The foundation of counting in the decimal system, it is the number of fingers on our two hands. Ten also represents the end of a journey and a return to unity.

Magical Symbols

I'm sure you've seen pictures of magical dolls that are absolutely covered with arcane symbols, but in my opinion this is often just done to make it look like some serious occult working rather than actually being necessary. Symbols can be powerful – but use ones that are relevant to you rather than just ones you've looked up in a book or online without having any cultural connection. Think about what is meaningful to you personally, such as symbols in common usage with folkloric significance such as hearts, stars, four-leaf clovers, horseshoes and bells. You can draw, paint or embroider these on or attach small bead charms. If the symbols of astrology, tarot, planetary magic, the elements or other esoteric traditions are meaningful to you, then use them by all means.

Anointing Your Doll

You can anoint your doll with oil or water to boost your intention. Pure olive oil is one I often use. It represents abundance, wisdom, fertility, purity, victory and peace, which is good for many types of spellwork. You can also add a few drops of any pure essential oil you feel might add to the effect. Some types of doll could be damaged or marked by oils, in which case use water. This can be blessed water, water from a sacred spring, dew collected on an auspicious morning or you can use a herbal infusion.

To increase the connection to a person, you can anoint your doll with bodily fluids. This doesn't have to be anything gross

– the sweat on your hands as you craft your doll will work. If you want to add to that you could anoint your doll with a little saliva, a spilled tear (if appropriate for the spell) or a drop of blood if, like me, you tend to prick your fingers whenever you are sewing. I'm sure suggestions for sex magic will come readily to mind – and are powerful as magical ingredients – but don't do anything you are uncomfortable with, just a little kiss can do the trick.

Bags of Extras

Although herbs and dried flowers can be put inside the bodies of some poppets, that isn't always possible. If you want to add these things after a poppet has been made, one way is to make a tiny bag, pouch or wrap and attach it. Tiny drawstring bags can be tied to poppets or you can bind wrapped bundles in place with wool, thread or ribbon. One simple trick is to use dried herbal tea mixtures of the kind that come in strong teabags with string attached. The best quality ones have bags that are hard wearing enough not to fall apart in your teacup – or around your poppet. Tie it under any clothing your poppet has or securely bind it to the outside with extra ribbon or wool to stop it flopping about.

Practical Crafting: Embellish Your Doll

Pick one or two dolls you made in the previous exercise and practise adornment styles. Add features, symbols or words as you see fit to familiarise yourself with the techniques. Being able to do this with ease will leave you free to concentrate on your magical intent when you come to make a poppet as part of a spell.

Chapter 5

The Prickly Subject of Pins and Thorns

In popular culture, poppets and pins go together like a witch and her cat – not entirely without reason. Strictly speaking, when a witch inserts pins, thorns or other small pointed objects into a poppet they are using them to focus their energy and magical intent. This can be done for all sorts of purposes. It can be done for healing – visualising the pins as acupuncture needles or surgical instruments, for example. It can be done for love magic, viewing the poppet as being pierced by cupid's arrow. In fact, some of the very earliest examples of effigy magic were used for love or lust while in other cases models were made of those who had died and were pinned so their spirits wouldn't rise from the grave to haunt the living.

In reality, you can use effigy magic of all kinds without anything sharp or prickly – as I hope I have already shown. However, historically pins and thorns have been used in conjunction with magical dolls a great deal. From most times and cultures there are examples of effigies being stuck with pins to cause pain to another. Sticking a pin into a picture or effigy of someone you dislike with the idea of hurting them is an obvious technique. Psychologically, it works – even if you don't believe it has any magical effect. It can make you feel better to take your anger out on something inanimate when you know you shouldn't stick anything pointy into a real person. Sometimes that's cathartic. But, if you are reading this book, I hope you are aware that sticking a pin in a magical doll as part of a spell has exactly the same intention as doing it to the person in the flesh. I'm not saying all spells work all the time, but don't do a spell assuming – or hoping – it won't. Magic, especially curses, should be taken very seriously. I go into ethics in more detail in chapter 6. Please read that and think about it carefully if you are contemplating casting any spell for harm. In this chapter, what I'm going to be discussing is how pins and thorns can be used in the crafting of poppets, fixing correspondences, directing energy and for healing as well as for wishing pain on anyone.

Why Pins?

Historically, pins are a common ingredient in many types of spell, quite apart from poppets. For example, there's an old love spell in which you pin four bay leaves to your pillow in order to dream of your future beloved. Pins were traditionally put into witch bottles – along with urine and various other things – which were then buried under the doors of houses or by the chimney to protect the inhabitants against curses. There are traditional alternatives to pins. Many witches prefer sharp thorns. Blackthorn is commonly used. In fact, some people say blackthorn is preferable to pins – especially for curses. Rose thorns can be used for love spells, while cactus thorns could represent endurance to hardship and the ability to survive in tough conditions. I've seen small nails stuck in poppets and I've used cocktail sticks too. Use what you have available, but if you have plenty of choice, think about what each symbolises or means to you personally and pick the most appropriate.

Pins and Craftwork

One important thing to bear in mind when making a poppet is that the magic isn't fully active unless and until you enchant it or bring it to life as part of your spell or ritual. While you are making the doll, it is a work in progress. So, if you pin two pieces of fabric together before sewing them up with a sharp needle or use a knife to help mould wax or clay, you are not causing anyone any harm unless you accidentally prick your own finger or have some other unfortunate crafting mishap. (By the way, if you do prick your finger while making a poppet that represents yourself, before you put a sticky plaster on it, remember a little of your own blood is a great bodily fluid for forging a physical link – although also be aware of health and safety issues relating to blood.)

You can also insert pins or other objects into the doll while you make it to represent conditions you want to deal with. After the doll has been activated, remove the pins or other items to represent a wound, addiction or attachment going away.

Pins and small nails can be used as crafting tools to carve features such as eyes and mouths or other symbols or words onto clay or wax. The fine point of a pin is better for small details than a big boline blade – boline is the name for a witch's dedicated crafting knife.

Magical Attachments

Pins are great for joining things. That's what they are designed for and you can use them to do that magically as well as in mundane life. You can happily fix flowers, leaves, pieces of paper, felt shapes, charms or whatever to your poppet with a pin as part of a spell to attach whatever the item symbolises to the person in question. Intention is everything. You could pin a heart shape onto a poppet as part of a spell to attract love – while sticking a pin or three into a heart shape already sewn onto a poppet might symbolise heartbreak *a la* three of swords in tarot.

Directing Energy

Pins can be used as miniature wands or athames (magical knives used purely for ritual purposes and the companion to the boline) that witches use to direct energy. If you want to focus a specific energy into a poppet, by all means use the perfect tool to pinpoint exactly where you want that energy to go. If you need to push the pin into the poppet, perhaps because you want that energy to get right inside the person in question, do so. No harm is wished, so no harm will be done.

Healing

I have already mentioned that you can put pins or other objects into poppets while you are making them. They can represent wounds or diseases that need healing. Then, after the doll has been activated, you can remove them to represent that wound or disease being cured or healing taking place. You can also visualise pins as performing surgery or acupuncture on a poppet to relieve pain, lance the symptoms of a disease or cut away something that needs to go. That technique can be used to help tackle physical or emotional issues.

Pain

Of course it is possible to stick a pin into a poppet after it has been activated with a wish to cause someone pain. I describe some historic examples in detail in chapter 8. But, before you go ahead and curse someone, please read the next chapter.

Practical Magic: Working with Pins

This is an exercise in directing energy and pinning it to your poppet with the idea of holding the magical intention in place. Take the basic handkerchief poppet that you made in chapter 2 and find a pin. If you like, you can use a pin with a pretty top like an old-fashioned hat pin, but you can use a simple dressmaker's pin. Repeat the candle and poppet spell, but this time, as the candle is burning, hold the pin as though it is a mini wand. First point it towards the candle flame, then move it to point towards the doll. While you do this, visualise directing the magic into the doll. Hold this intention for a few moments, then secure the pin to the edge of the handkerchief, visualising fixing the spell in place. Say: *'By the power of this pin, I secure this spell.'*

You can leave the pin in place until your spell has worked. When it has, you can remove the pin and say: *'The spell is done; I release the magic as I free this pin.'*

Chapter 6

Ethics, Cursing and Assertive Magic

The practice of sticking pins or thorns in poppets or other effigies of others in order to cause them suffering by means of sympathetic magic is old and widespread. The Museum of Witchcraft and Magic has many poppets of different kinds in its collection. While some were evidently used for healing or other benign purposes, most have obviously been used with the intention of causing hurt. However, I am absolutely not using those facts to argue that modern witches should be quick to curse. In fact, I would encourage anyone contemplating a curse to think about it very carefully and weigh up all the options available.

Points of View on Cursing

Many modern pagans believe it is unethical or counterproductive to use magic for harm under any circumstances, while others – particularly those following more traditional witchcraft paths – believe cursing is sometimes necessary, or at least that understanding how to curse is an important part of a witch's knowledge.

During WWII, pincushions were made in the likeness of Hitler. Many of those sewing to 'make do and mend' would have happily stuck a pin into the Nazi dictator's bottom and wished him ill. The Museum of Witchcraft and Magic has one on display. Using this as an example, while researching for this book, I asked the question on several pagan social media groups: *'Would you stick pins in a tyrant's effigy?'*

The topic generated a lot of discussion, so I thought it was worthwhile summarising the findings. Seventy-five people responded with an answer that could be classified as 'yes', 'no' or 'undecided/only to heal them', although there were many more other responses – some of which I'm not going to repeat here because I don't want to get sued. Of the 75, 38 said they would stick pins in a tyrant's effigy, 21 said they wouldn't and 16 said they were undecided or would only use pins to heal the tyrant – possibly psychologically. Adding the number of those who wouldn't prick a poppet to those who were undecided or would only heal gives a figure of 37. To sum up, more people in the admittedly small survey would happily stick pins in a tyrant's effigy (38) than would not or might not (37). Obviously this was more of a quick vox pop than a sociological study, but here are a few representative comments from those who replied:

Hell yes!

It's all down to personal ethics I guess and while I'm happy to live in peace and harmony with all, all may not be happy to live in peace and harmony with me, in which case I will defend myself and those I love!

'Do what you will but harm none' [The Wiccan Rede] comes to my mind all the time.

What is less harm: stopping one tyrant bringing war and death to innocents or allowing said tyrant to cause unimagined horrors?

Hmmmm not sure. Take for example a person whose negative behaviour is aggravated by mental and physical anxieties and stress. If you employ magic that increases these symptoms are you not partly responsible for escalating those negative behaviours?

I would normally say no, but desperate times call for desperate measures...

No. Energy goes where attention grows. Remove energy from negativity by focusing on positivity.

I do have one rule before [I] do anything drastic...I give myself (when possible) at least a day or two to calm down, think it through...and if the desire is still there, or the threat is still there...well screw it...I'm goin' in.

While it seems many contemporary witches are prepared to stick pins into poppets to cause pain in extreme circumstances, I suspect if the question had been whether they would do it to someone who had merely annoyed them, the number saying yes would have been considerably smaller. Modern sensibilities in witchcraft are different from those of our ancestors.

One of the comments above mentions the Wiccan Rede, which states: 'An it harm none, do what ye will.' This is found in the Wiccan *Book of Shadows* and probably dates back to the mid 20th century, when the *Book of Shadows* was being compiled by Gerald Gardner and Doreen Valiente. The word 'Rede' means 'advice' rather than 'rule', but many Wiccans take seriously the concept of never doing magic that will harm. Not all witches are Wiccans, but nevertheless the general ethos of the Rede is quite prevalent in modern paganism.

Another term commonly mentioned in discussions about cursing is the 'Law of Threefold Return'. It is the idea that whatever you do magically will come back to you threefold. This is another Wiccan concept, but was devised more recently than the Rede and does not appear in any of Gerald Gardner's early writings on ethics, and he was the father of Gardnerian Wicca. Luth Adams, in *The Book of Mirrors*, researched the origins of the threefold return concept and discovered that the closest Gerald Gardner came to that was: 'Learn, in witchcraft, thou must ever return triple.' That quote is from *High Magic's Aid*, published in 1949, and could be read as the opposite of the way the Law of

Threefold Return is currently understood. It could suggest that if, as a witch, someone does something to you, you should pay them back in kind threefold.

Those who follow more traditional witchcraft paths tend not to be so reluctant to curse. Many believe cursing is sometimes necessary or at least that learning how to curse is an important part of a witch's training even if they never curse anyone. Some go so far as to say that if you can't curse, then you can't cure. Cecil Williamson, who founded the Museum of Witchcraft and Magic and was himself a spellcaster-for-hire, was frequently asked to perform both curses and counter-curses. According to Judith Noble, who spoke about Cecil Williamson's practices at the museum's annual conference in 2017, said he had told her he only turned down requests for 'black magic' if the person asking was mentally unstable.

I would never tell another witch what they must or must not do, but my personal view is that physically hurting anyone – whether by magical or mundane means – is best left for self-defence and last resort, when all other means of getting justice have failed. My preferred type of spell is what I call assertive magic. Assertiveness is being self-assured and confident without being aggressive. Assertiveness techniques generally have the goal of getting you what you want, but also leaving everyone content with the final outcome – a win-win situation.

Here is an example of a spell of that kind that I cast a few years ago. I was working as a temp in an office where one manager was disliked by the staff. A couple of my co-workers, knowing I was a witch, asked if I could do some magic to get rid of him. The next full moon, I cast a spell that the manager would be sent a very attractive job offer by another company a long way away. A few weeks after that I was temping in the same office again and learnt that indeed the manager had taken a new job for a distant firm. Success – and everyone was happy with the result. I was pleased with that spell because not only was no one harmed, the manager had complete free will over whether he accepted the job offer or not.

The issue of whether it is ethical to do a spell that affects another person's free will is another controversial issue. Some witches say you should never do magic to affect another's ability to make their own choices about what they do. Again, I tend to think that if someone is behaving badly and upsetting or hurting people and all mundane methods of stopping them have failed, then it is acceptable to use a little magical help to bind them or otherwise try to stop them repeating antisocial behaviour.

Some people say that you should always ask permission of a person before casting a spell on them or for them. Well, again that is a matter of debate, but in general if you are casting a spell with the intention of helping a person – for healing, job searching, finding love, fertility or whatever – I would recommend asking them first. Some people don't want magical help and it is polite to respect their wishes. Sometimes it isn't possible to ask. For example, if they have been rushed into hospital unconscious. In that case I would do what I felt was best, but every witch must act according to their own sense of propriety.

Some of the spells in the following chapters are controversial; included for information purposes and not as suggestions to try out. What I would recommend is to tread as lightly as possible when you cast any spell to affect the world with your will and consider the potential outcome before picking up your pin.

Exercise

Think how you would answer the question: *'Would you stick pins in a tyrant's effigy?'*

Chapter 7

Rituals to Enchant Your Poppet

Without enchantment, a poppet is just a doll. It might look the part, it might even be full of correspondences, symbolism and connections, but the magic isn't complete. This chapter describes a basic ritual to bring your poppet to magical life; to awaken its inherent properties and charge it with purpose. However, you should decide what you want to wish for before you even start to make your doll – and definitely before you bring it to magical life. Ideally, write down the wording of your wish and have it with you as you cast your spell.

Preparing for Spellwork and Casting a Circle

Before moving on to the details of poppet rituals, I'm briefly going to cover the preparation work I'd recommend doing before casting any spells. If you are an experienced witch, you can skip this part, but as this is a beginners' book I'm including it. Here's a brief preparation checklist:

- Gather all the equipment and materials you need.
- Cleanse yourself and the space in which you are going to work.
- Cast a circle.
- Welcome the elements and any powers or spirits you feel are appropriate (actually, this stage is optional for spellwork, but many witches do it).
- Raise magical energy. There are many ways of doing this, but the most common methods are: chanting or singing; drumming or other music; dancing or walking around your circle; channelling energy from the earth and/or sky.

The first stage – gathering everything you need before starting – is kind of obvious. The other stages vary from tradition to tradition and if you have your own system, use that. Otherwise, here are some simple ways of going about it.

Cleansing yourself can be done by having a bath to which a pinch of salt has been added. If that isn't possible, mix up some salty water and gently sprinkle a little over yourself. As you do that, say: 'May my body and mind be cleansed.'

Physically clean the space you're going to work in – traditionally this is done with a broom. Then sprinkle a little salty water over the space and say: 'May this space be cleansed.'

Circles are cast to create a special place in which to work magic – to contain the energy and keep out unwanted influences. Obviously your circle isn't physical enough to keep out people or pets, it is just intended to keep negative energy away. You can cast a circle by walking around the boundary of your space clockwise (deosil or sunwise) while visualising creating a protective barrier as you walk, or you can visualise drawing a circle around yourself in the air using a wand or athame. You can say: 'I cast this circle to be a safe and sacred space within which to work magic. May it protect and contain all within.'

Once the circle is cast many witches like to welcome the elements of air, fire, water and earth, although for simple spellwork this is optional. If you want to do it, turn to each compass direction and invite the element associated with each one. Welcome air in the east, fire in the south, water in the west and earth in the north. You can say: 'Hail and welcome to the element of XXX.'

In some traditions, practitioners welcome the earth, sea and sky; ancestors; deities they honour; spirits of place or other spirits or powers, but only do this if it feels appropriate to you.

Raising energy is something I would recommend doing as it will help charge your spell. Use a method you feel most drawn to. There are many pagan chants that are great for raising energy. If you don't know any then do an online search and learn one or think of a song you know that has suitable words. You could simply repeat over and over: *'Energy raised!'* Rhythmic drumming is great – if you don't own a percussion instrument you can improvise by banging on anything that makes a noise. Walking or dancing around your circle at least three times is good – and less noisy if you don't want the neighbours to hear you chanting, singing or drumming on an old saucepan. Another way of raising energy is to sit still, close your eyes and visualise drawing earth energy up from the core of the planet, or drawing the energy of the moon or sun down from the heavens, then visualising it filling your circle. You can use a combination of techniques.

This basic set-up – or something similar – is what I recommend before any type of spellwork or ritual, including the enchantment of poppets and magical dolls. Ideally, I would suggest making the poppet within a circle as well as enchanting it there. However, if you need bright light or specialist equipment to make the doll of your choice, which wouldn't be conducive for the magical atmosphere of a circle, it's okay to make the doll's body first and only cast your circle and enchant it later.

Enchanting Your Poppet

Here is a ritual to forge the magical connection between a poppet and an individual. The essential magical part of linking a poppet to the person it represents is naming it. As in chapter 2, you could simply pick up your poppet and say three times: *'I name you XXX.'* However, you can improve on that.

First consecrate the doll by anointing it with blessed water, water from a sacred spring or a little olive oil. To bless any fluid, pour a little into a small dish, put it on your altar and ask the deity or deities you honour, or the spirits of the place, to bless it. You could say: *'Powers and deities I hold most sacred, I ask you to bless this water/oil.'*

Dab a little onto the head of the doll, saying: *'May this doll be blessed and consecrated.'*

Then you need to name the doll. If it is to represent yourself or another individual, you will give it the same name as them. You can call on the elements, spirits and powers you have invited to your circle, as well as any deities you honour, to add power. You can make up your own words or say something like: *'By the deities I honour, by the powers of moon and sun, by the elements of earth, air, fire and water, by the force of spirit and by magic rite, I call you to life. I name you XXX.'*

Finally, blow a puff of air onto the mouth of the poppet and visualise it taking its first breath and coming to life.

Now you can use your poppet as a focus for all kinds of spellwork; what you do to the poppet you are also doing to the person it represents. There are suggestions for specific kinds of spells later, but you can simply chant, speak or visualise your wishes for the person while holding the poppet.

Candle magic works well alongside poppets. As in the candle spell exercise in chapter 2, you can inscribe your wish on a candle, light it and place it so the light falls on the doll. If you want to take candle magic further, I recommend my book *Pagan Portals – Candle Magic*, also published by Moon Books.

Ending the Rite and Opening the Circle

When you have completed your spellwork, you need to bring the rite to a close and open the circle. Again, if you are an experienced witch you will know your own way of doing that, but below are basic details for those who want them.

It is polite to give thanks to any elements, spirits or deities you earlier welcomed. That can be done by raising a toast to them with a drink – alcoholic or otherwise – and offering shared bread or cake as well as saying thanks in words. Witches often call this 'cakes and wine'. After that, say goodbye to the deities, spirits and elements in the reverse order to the way you welcomed them, then walk around your circle widdershins (anti-clockwise) – or do an anti-clockwise motion around it with your wand or athame – and say: 'The rite is done, the circle is open.'

After you have done any spells, rituals or energy work it is important to ground yourself, otherwise you can still feel a little spacey. The witchiest way to do that is to have a feast after the rite, but something like a cup of tea and a biccie will do if you are short of time. Failing that, place your feet firmly on the ground, wiggle your toes and concentrate on your physical connection to the earth.

Care of Magical Dolls

Once your poppet has been enchanted, treat it carefully. Where you place it or keep it will vary depending on its purpose and nature. You might want it on your altar or always have it with you in your pocket or bag. You can place one somewhere associated with the intention of the spell: in the bedroom if you are looking for extra passion; on your desk to help you pass your exams; on top of your CV if you want a new job. Make sure your poppet is kept clean and tidy – give it a dust, make sure it hasn't fallen over and clutter hasn't built up around it.

If you don't want to leave your poppet on display, perhaps because you live in a shared house with people who don't have the same beliefs as you, keep it somewhere safe. You could get or make a special box or bag to store the doll in, then hide it away from prying eyes.

Deeper into the Magic of Poppets and Dolls

Here is a bit more in-depth theory about the different ways in which effigies such as poppets and magical dolls can be used. Being aware of the subtle differences can be useful to bear in mind when deciding the appropriate way to make, enchant and use them – and later dispose of them. Some of the different types have been described already; some will be gone into in more detail in later chapters.

- A true poppet is created to completely represent an individual. It effectively *is* that person for the purposes of magic. In Irish folklore this is sometimes called a 'fetch', meaning a supernatural double of a living person. Although it won't look exactly like them, it will be created to symbolically represent them as closely as possible. For example, you could attempt to get as close as possible to the colour of their hair, eyes and skin when you make the doll. You might mark it with their name and things to represent their gender, age or astrological sign. It should include something like their hair or nail clippings or a photograph. You then use the poppet when you want to affect the person in any way.
- A second type of poppet represents an aspect of a person you wish to give a magic boost to. It still represents them, but with certain aspects emphasised. This is a good type of poppet to make of yourself to help you through specific tasks. A way do to this is to make the doll in a colour that has the right symbolism and associations (see chapter 3). After naming your poppet in the rite to enchant it, you could add the intention of the poppet with the words: '*I charge you to XXX (boost my psychic powers or help me ask my boss for a raise*, for example).'
- Magical helper dolls, as described in chapter 1, don't represent a specific individual; they are more like companions who assist us, possibly throughout our lives. You can give them whatever names you like or seem appropriate. I have a beanbag frog helper doll I call Kermit.
- Guardian dolls can be designed as protection spells. They might be intended to stay in a specific place to watch over it and keep it safe. They can look scary to frighten off any other threat. One example is kitchen witch dolls (see

chapter 8). Again, you can give these any name that seems appropriate.

- Dolls can be created to represent deities or other figures from mythology that you wish to honour in your spiritual practice – perhaps to place on your altar. You should cast a circle and invite the deity in question to give their blessings for this (see chapter 10).

- Dolls of remembrance – you can create dolls in memory or respect of ancestors or others who have passed. You can use them to help communicate with a beloved relative who has died or simply to honour their memory (see chapter 11). These should be named after the ancestor.

- Seasonal dolls: many folklore practices around the world involve dolls that represent the spirit of the season. These include Brigid dolls for Imbolc or Candlemas, corn dollies, straw dogs and Yule tree fairies. Some, such as corn dollies, don't always look like dolls at all even though they are called dollies. These would be created in traditional ways that don't have to involve casting a circle or naming them (see chapter 12).

- In many traditions, dolls can be used as spirit houses. Sometimes this relates to seasonal rites – such as creating a home for the spirit of the fields to live in throughout the winter, to be placed into the soil before crops are planted again in the spring. Sometimes the spirit of someone who has passed will take residence in a doll, either by invitation or choice. For more on this, see chapters 11, 12 and 13.

Exercise

List as many reasons you can think of for making a magical doll for yourself.

Chapter 8

More Spells with Poppets and Magical Dolls

Here are some ideas for spells using poppets and magical dolls for a variety of specific purposes including luck, healing, job searching, love, fertility, communication, justice, confidence, happiness and success. There are also a few curses towards the end.

Luck and Success

Lucky black cat charm

As a talisman to bring good luck, make a black cat-shaped poppet from felt, small enough to keep in your pocket or bag. Inside the cat put a mixture of herbs and items associated with luck such as an acorn and dried heather, clover or mint. Add a few strands of your own hair – and a few strands of fur fallen from your own cat if you have one. Put a yellow or gold ribbon around the neck of the cat and to it hang a small metal charm associated with luck, such as a four-leaf clover. Enchant the cat on a Sunday when the moon is full or nearly full. Say: *'I name you my good luck cat and charge you to attract the best that can happen in all things.'*

Healing

Doll spells have traditionally been used to help heal humans and animals since ancient times and even today can complement medical treatment. However, please be aware that magic should never be used as a substitute for medical or psychological help from a qualified expert.

Laying on hands

Make a poppet to represent the person who needs healing. Either hold the poppet in your hands or hold your hands a centimetre or two above the poppet – where the aura would be – and visualise love and healing flowing into them. Once you have enchanted the poppet, you can do a laying-on of hands as often as you like – it doesn't have to be inside a sacred space or circle.

Healing guardian angels

Make a poppet to represent the person. Also make four paper guardian angels by folding a piece of card or paper in two and drawing one half of the outline of an angel against the fold. Cut out the angel through the fold so it makes an entire figure. This should stand up if the fold is left slightly creased. Using this as a template, make three more. Name and charge each angel, then stand them around the poppet to watch over it. You can leave this set up on your altar or another place where it won't be disturbed. Although I have called these guardian angels, they could be fairies, spirits or representations of ancestors depending on the belief system or request of the person who is ill.

Removing the hurt

A pin or thorn can be placed in a wax poppet as you make it, but before you enchant or name it, to represent a wound or disease that needs healing. After you have named and enchanted the poppet, remove the pin. Say: '*As I remove this pin, may the ailment go.*'

Sleep well doll

Make a soft, fabric doll out of blue material. Inside it put dried hops and lavender or camomile. Keep it by your pillow or hang it over your bed to help you sleep.

Animal healing

Make a poppet in the shape of the animal out of orange felt or the colour of the animal in question. If it is for a cat, stuff it with catnip. Another herb suitable for animal poppets is mint. If it is a furry pet, put a little fur inside the poppet before sewing it up, which you can collect through stroking or grooming. Then use the Laying-on-Hands spell, above, with the animal healing poppet.

Fertility

Wedding day cork spell for fertility

If a couple are getting married or handfasted and have plans to start a family, save the corks from any bottles of wine opened at the wedding celebration. For this spell you need five corks – ideally two of them should be from Champagne or other sparkling wines, as these have tops that make great heads for poppets. Using four of the corks, make two full-size poppets using the instructions in chapter 3. Dress them as the couple in wedding garb. Use the fifth cork to make a baby poppet. Bind the three poppets together with green wool or ribbon and say: 'May this union be blessed with fertility.'

Cloth doll with baby doll inside

Make a white, green or pink fabric poppet to represent the woman who is planning to have a baby and a tiny poppet to represent the unborn child. Stuff the adult poppet with sunflower seeds, but leave enough room inside to later insert the baby poppet into the womb area and leave a small area unstitched. You can pin it shut to stop the seeds falling out if necessary. Do a ritual to name the adult poppet, then put the baby poppet inside and do the final stitches. Say: 'May you be blessed with fertility.'

To Cheer Your Mood

Cinderella doll of transformation

Here is some Cinderella fairy tale magic for transformation – perfect when you have the blues and want to be in the pink. Create a poppet that instead of having one head at the top and feet at the bottom, has two heads – one at either end. It should also have two sets of arms. Put a frowning expression at one end and a smile on the face at the other. Then make two circles the same size of stretchy fabric to form skirts. One should be blue fabric and the other pink. Make a hole in the centre of each, just wide enough to fit as a skirt around the middle of the doll and place them on it so that when the frowning head is upright, the blue skirt shows, but when the smiling face is upright, the pink skirt is on top. You might need to overstitch the edges of the skirt fabric if it frays, or trim it with pinking shears.

Enchant your doll and give it your name. Charge it to transform your sadness into happiness and your tears into smiles.

When you are feeling down, turn the doll frowning side up and tell it all your woes and problems. Spend as long as you need to do this. Then reverse the doll so the smiling face and pink skirt are showing. Ask the doll to help you smile and spend some time meditating with it, feeling the transformative magic change your mood.

Big hugs candle magic

Here's a little spell to give you a magical warm hug when you are feeling down. It originally appeared in my book *Pagan Portals – Candle Magic*.

Find a clear glass jar or candle holder with plenty of room inside for a tea-light, then measure a wide strip of paper long enough to wrap around the jar. Cut a chain of paper dolls from the strip. The way you do this is to fold the paper into pleats and then, with the paper folded, draw half a doll shape on the top fold, with half a head and body against one edge of the paper and the hands and feet touching against the other edge. Cut out the shapes through all the layers of paper and unfold to reveal your row of dolls holding hands. You can draw or paint features and clothes on the dolls or you can leave them plain. Tape the dolls around the outside of the jar or candle holder.

Take the tea-light out of its container for a moment and rub the candle between your hands a few times, then put it back into the metal container before popping it into the jar. Light the candle and visualise yourself feeling hugged and loved. You can reuse your chain of hugging dolls and jar as often as you like.

Spell to get rid of unwanted emotion

It is natural to sometimes feel anger, frustration, jealousy or get the blues, but this is a good spell to try if you aren't feeling quite the way you would like.

Make a doll from salt dough. Knead your unwanted anger, frustration or other unwanted feelings into the dough as you make it. Shape the dough into a doll. Name it by saying: *'I name you my anger (or other unwanted emotion).'* Bake it hard in the oven, then leave it to cool. Then, break the doll into pieces – you can smash it up into crumbs if you like – and say: *'I release you, anger (etc), you are dust.'* Then dispose of the pieces, ideally by burning them in an open fire, burying them, or putting them into the recycling. Remember that salt can harm plants and animals, so dispose of it thoughtfully.

Guardian Dolls

Guardian dolls help protect your home, garden and other spaces. The two below are designed to look just a little bit scary, because scary figures and images have traditionally been used to deter unwanted intruders – real or in spirit form.

Kitchen witches

A kitchen witch – as well as being a real-life witch who brews up magic in the heart of her home – is the name given to a doll that looks like an old crone flying on a broomstick. These magical charms, or poppets, are supposed to ward off evil. The tradition comes from northern Europe, although one hint that they may have at one time been an English folk custom appears in the will of a John Crudgington, of Newton, Worfield, Shropshire, dated 1599. In it, he included among his household possessions 'one witche in the kytchyn'.

This one is relatively simple to make.

You need:
Green felt
Black stretchy velvet
Some dark brown wool
A green pipe-cleaner
Two small black buttons
Stuffing material (ideally use a combination of dried leaves associated with protection such as: ash, blackthorn, elder, hawthorn, hazel, nettle, rosemary, rowan, sage, willow or witch hazel)
Sewing needle
Black and green sewing thread
A short hazel or ash stick (or a wooden dowel)
Some short birch twiglets

Make the head of the witch by cutting two circles of green felt, 5cm in diameter. Trim both circles into a witchy face in profile, with a hooked nose and upwardly pointing chin to one side. Overstitch around most of the face, leaving a gap at the neck. Fill the head with stuffing and then complete the outer stitching.

To make the body, fold the pipe-cleaner in two and stitch the middle of the pipe-cleaner to the bottom of the head.

To make a witch's cloak, cut a 20cm square of black stretchy velvet, then cut a very small hole in the middle of the square. Thread the pipe-cleaner ends through the hole and stitch the fabric to the bottom of the head around where the pipe-cleaner is attached.

To make a witch's hat, cut a triangle of black stretchy velvet, with each side 10cm. With right side facing, stitch two sides of the triangle, then turn it so the right side of the fabric is on the outside and the seam on the inside. Stitch the open edge of the hat around the witch's face.

Stitch the two buttons either side of the face as eyes and cut a bunch of strands of wool, 15-20cm long, for the hair. Stitch the middle of the bunch of wool to the top of the head, just in front of the edge of the hat. Let the strands fall loosely on either side of the face. Stitch a long loop of wool to the top of the head to hang the witch up from.

To make the broom, take the hazel or ash stick (or dowel) and tie the birch twiglets (or more strands of wool) to the bottom. Wrap both ends of the pipe-cleaner several times around the broom's middle so the cloak hangs down far enough to hide all the pipe-cleaner.

Do a ritual to enchant your witch. Cast a circle and say: *'Kitchen witch, I name you XXX. I charge you to guard my kitchen, my hearth and my home.'*

Hang your witch up by the kitchen door or back door to your home.

Scarecrows

While kitchen witches are guardians of the hearth and home, scarecrows guard the fields and gardens. Although they are traditionally made in springtime to keep birds from sown seeds, you can make a scarecrow doll at any time and charge it to guard your outdoor spaces. Scarecrows are usually made from old clothing stuffed with straw, with a stuffed pillow for a head, then tied to a long pole. If you only have a window box or a balcony with plants, you can make a miniature version of a scarecrow, cutting small clothes and a head out of old garments or felt. Tie the scarecrow to a stick and put it in a flowerpot full of soil.

Guardian Angel or Fairy Godmother Doll

You need
Cardboard
Gold or silver paint, paper or fabric
Red paper or fabric
Ribbon

Who wouldn't want a guiding spirit, guardian angel, fairy godmother or embodiment of their higher self watching over them? You can make a doll to represent this.

Cut out two identical angel or fairy shapes from corrugated cardboard. In the centre of one of these, cut out a heart shape. Either paint the shapes silver or gold, or cover them with gold paper or fabric. Fold the ribbon in two. Glue the two angel shapes together with red paper or fabric sandwiched in the middle so it shows through the heart-shaped hole and the ends of the ribbon sandwiched at the top of the head. When the glue is dry, hang the angel or fairy where you need her.

Enchant your guardian by saying: *'Guardian angel (or fairy), I ask you to watch over me, keep me safe and guide me for the best in all that happens.'*

You can also make these for friends and relatives and give them as presents for Yule.

Love and Romance Spells

Gingerbread figure of loveliness
In general I would recommend doing spells to make yourself

feel more attractive rather than casting spells on other people to make them desire you. This one involves making a sweet gingerbread person using honey, cinnamon and ginger.

You need
70g butter
50g brown sugar
1½ tbsp honey
175g plain flour
½ tsp baking powder
1 tsp ground ginger
½ tsp ground cinnamon

Heat your oven to 200C/180C fan/gas 6. Melt the butter, sugar and honey in a pan, stirring clockwise and visualising the sweetness of the mixture. Mix the flour, baking powder and spices in a bowl. Stir in the butter and mix into a dough, again using clockwise motions. Visualise stirring the properties of loveliness into the mixture. Say three times: *'Sugar and spice and all things nice, like this cake am I in a trice.'*

Leave the sweet and spicy dough to cool, then put it on a floured surface and roll it out to about ½cm thick. Cut out person shapes using a gingerbread cutter – or go freehand if you prefer, using a sharp knife or your boline. The mixture should make about nine small gingerbread people or five larger ones.

Put the gingerbread people onto a baking tray lined with baking paper. Bake them for 12 minutes. When they are golden in colour, turn off the heat and leave them to cool.

Once the gingerbread people are baked and cooled, pick the very nicest looking one. You can give it a smiling face with icing if you like, but that isn't essential.

Cast a circle and enchant your gingerbread person saying: *'I name you sweet, desirable, lovely and gorgeous.'* Then, while still in the circle, eat the gingerbread, perhaps with a glass of mead (known as the honeymoon drink) and say: 'As you become part of me, so I become as you – sweet, desirable, lovely and gorgeous.'

You can eat up all the other gingerbread people too, or share them with friends.

Valentine's Day doll

Valentine's Day is the time of year when it is easiest to tell someone you love them. Rather than just buying a card from a shop, here is a doll you can make to give as a special gift – adding extra oomph to it with magic.

Make a small fabric doll. When you are choosing what fabric to use, you could buy new material in red or pink silk, or reuse something, perhaps from a beautiful dress you love that has seen better days. Inside the doll put dried lavender and/or rose petals, cinnamon and (optionally) a little frankincense. Cut out a heart shape from a contrasting piece of fabric and stitch this to the outside of the doll. Embroider or write on the doll: 'Be My Valentine.'

Enchant the doll on a Friday, which is sacred to Venus, Goddess of Love and say: 'Venus hear this wish of mine, that (X) should be my Valentine.'

Give it to the one you love on Valentine's Day.

Wedding or handfasting dolls

These make a lovely wedding gift – although it is polite to first ask the couple if they want the spell done for them.

Make poppets to represent the bride and groom out of wooden spoons, which were traditionally given as tokens of love in parts of the UK. Dress them in appropriate attire for a wedding or handfasting, which is a pagan wedding in which the couple's hands are symbolically tied together with cord.

Cast a circle and name the poppets as the couple, then perform a mini handfasting ceremony for the dolls, binding them together by the hands with green cord and wishing them a long and happy union. Say: *'I bind X and X in love. May their union be happy and give them both all that they desire. So mote it be.'*

You can invite the friends, family and wedding guests to tie on ribbons or charms and make a wish for them as they do so – either when the spell is being cast or on the wedding day itself before you give it to the newly-weds.

Dolls to Boost Your Magic Powers

Dream divination doll

This is a more advanced version of the sleep well doll. Make a soft, fabric doll out of blue or white material and embroider or draw moon symbols on the outside. Inside the doll put dried lavender plus, optionally, sandalwood, mugwort or wormwood. If you cannot find dried ingredients, you can add a drop or two of essential oil mixed with a little olive oil to the herb mix. (Do not use mugwort if you are pregnant.) Enchant the doll on a Monday and ask the Lady of the Moon to bless the doll, then charge it to give you dreams of insight and prophecy. Keep the doll by your pillow or hang it over your bed.

Careers, Work and Job Searching

Dressed for the part

To help you get the job you want, make a cardboard cut-out dress-up doll as described in chapter 3, then draw and cut out paper clothes that are right for your desired career. Cast a circle, name the doll as yourself, then put the clothes on the doll, saying: *'I dress you and empower you for the job you are to do. So mote it be.'*

Wealth and Money

A witch who I respected greatly used to say that the path to material riches ran in the opposite direction to that for spiritual growth. I don't entirely agree. It's a lot easier to be serene if you aren't worrying about how to pay the bills. However, it is true that money spells are difficult to make work and they can behave in odd ways. I once cast a spell to get cash. For the next week I kept finding loose coppers in the street, old coat pockets and the back of the sofa. I must have gained all of 50p! Nevertheless, money spells are frequently asked for, so here are a couple.

For long-term financial improvement

This is a spell designed to improve your wealth over the course of a year, which you can use with a poppet made to represent yourself. You need a poppet, a small purse with a handle or drawstring, a gold or silver coloured coin and a citrine crystal, which is the stone of prosperity. Cast the spell on a sunny day or on the night of a full moon.

Cleanse the citrine, coins and purse by washing them or sprinkling them with salty water if washing isn't suitable. Hold up the purse and say: *'I charge this purse to store/My saved wealth/ And bring me more.'*

Then, place the coin and the citrine stone into the purse and say: *'Bring me silver/Bring me gold/Bring me riches/Manifold.'*

Tie or hang the purse to the poppet. Put them on a sunny windowsill. Every week, put a further cleansed coin into the purse and repeat the charm. Do not take any of the items out until a year and a day have passed. By that time, you should have noticed that your financial situation has improved. Even if it hasn't, you have a purse full of savings that you should use to treat yourself.

Spell for immediate need

If you suddenly need a specific amount of money for a particular purpose – perhaps to repair your car or home or pay an unexpected bill – try this.

Make a small poppet coloured gold, orange or green, stuff it with a photocopy or other facsimile of a bank note and a mixture of basil, thyme or allspice. Cast a circle and enchant the poppet, naming it *'Money, not greed, in time of need.'* Place the poppet on a piece of white paper and draw on the paper the thing you need as though it has been paid for and completed – so a working car, a repaired home, a bill marked paid etc. As you do this, visualise the thing you want to happen coming true. Leave the poppet and picture in a sunny spot or where the light of the moon will fall. When your problem is resolved remove the doll, thank it and decommission it (see chapter 9).

Communication

Make a poppet of the person you want to communicate with. Give it eyes, ears and a mouth. Stuff it with the herbs marjoram and/or thyme. Dress it in orange or tie a bow of orange ribbon or wool around it. Put a little geranium oil into a diffuser or anoint the poppet with a few drops of geranium oil mixed with olive oil. Name the poppet then talk to it as you would talk to the person. Visualise their side of the conversation in response to your words. Alternatively, or if you find it difficult to visualise a conversation with this person, write a letter to the person in blue ink. Write down all that you want to say to them. Dab a little geranium oil mixed with olive oil on the corner of the paper. Fold the finished letter up and tie it to the poppet with orange ribbon or wool.

Justice

Lady Justice is an allegorical personification of the moral force in judicial systems. She is often depicted blindfolded and carrying a set of scales and a sword. To petition for justice, make an effigy to represent Lady Justice – this could be done by drawing her as a paper or cardboard image and cutting out the shape, although you could also model a figure from wax or clay. You can wrap a ribbon around her eyes as a blindfold, while a small nail or long pin can be used for the sword. The scales could be carefully modelled from clay, cut out as a cardboard shape, or two buttons could be hung from string or cotton thread as a representation. To enchant her, cast a circle and name her as Lady Justice. Burn a purple candle and petition Lady Justice with your plea.

Charm for Travel

Historically, figures have been attached to boats and other methods of transport as charms to protect them and those within from disaster. Ship prow figureheads and car bonnet mascots are examples of this – my favourite is the Rolls-Royce Spirit of Ecstasy.

Today, I wouldn't recommend attaching a figure to the outside of your car, it is more likely to get stolen than protect you from anything, but you can make an amulet of protection to put inside a vehicle. For Christians, the St Christopher was the traditional amulet to wear when travelling. For a pagan alternative, the Greek God Apollo drives the chariot of the sun and can be called upon for aid. Roman charioteers would often seek the favour of Luna, Goddess of the moon, who was their dedicated protectress. An easy amulet to make is to cut out a small circle from gold-coloured card for the sun and a crescent moon shape of the same height from silver card. Stick the moon on top and to one edge of the sun disk. Draw a half-face of an eye, half a mouth and a half-nose on each of the sun and the moon, so they seem to join in the middle. Punch a hole at the top of the disk and put ribbon through it. Cast a circle and ask the blessings of the sun and moon for protection on your journeys, then hang the amulet in your vehicle.

Curses: Disempowering, Binding, Pricking, Banishing and Burning

Before casting any of these spells, read chapter 6 on ethics and decide what you actually want to achieve. Do you want justice? If so, do a spell for justice. Do you want to transform a difficult situation? Consider a spell that does that and makes everyone happy or that helps improve communication. If you believe casting a spell that negatively affects another person is the best way forward, then first consider one that does least harm, such as a spell to stop them being antisocial, rather than physically hurting them.

Frozen poppet

To 'freeze' a person so they cannot act or continue to act in a certain way, make a poppet representing that person and put it at the back of your freezer. Say: *'I freeze your actions, you are stopped.'*

To unfreeze them, take the doll out of the freezer and say: *'I release you from the ice.'*

Binding

Binding is a traditional way of preventing someone from acting in a specified way. Make a poppet to represent the person you want to bind, then take a length of cord and bind it around the poppet either three times or nine times. Say with each turn of the cord: *'I bind you XXX. I restrain you from XXX. You are bound until I release the cord.'* Tie the ends of the cord together with three or nine knots.

To unbind them, undo the knots and unwrap the cord saying: *'XXX I release you from your binding. I free you to act as you will. You are unbound.'*

Disempowering

Make a small poppet representing a caricature of person – with the idea that small things cannot be scary. The caricature should look harmless and humorous. Laughter is a great way of removing our own fear of anything and of rendering the thing we laugh at powerless to harm us. Deliberately laugh at the poppet and say: *'You are a joke. You are harmless. I laugh at you.*

You have no power over me!'

To prick a person's conscience

Do this if you want to prick a person's conscience into doing the right thing. Perhaps they have taken something that is yours and not returned it, despite you repeatedly asking them for it back, for example. Make a poppet of the person and lightly prick it with a pin. Say: *'I prick your conscience, XXX. May you feel the stings of remorse over what you have done until you put it right.'*

Banishing

In general, if I want someone to go away or leave me alone I prefer to do a spell that draws their attention elsewhere. If I want a nuisance neighbour to move, I might cast a spell that gives them the offer of a wonderful new home – or a wonderful new job – a long way away. Create a poppet of them and then write a miniature 'letter' on a piece of paper with words such as 'new home far away' or 'new job far away', then cast a circle and pin the letter to the doll, saying something like: *'May XXX receive the offer of a wonderful new home (or job), a long way from here.'* As I said earlier, that is assertive magic and everyone wins. However, if attempts at that kind of spell have failed and you really want them to go away, you could up the ante and physically send the poppet far away. The traditional method was to throw it in a fast-moving river, but nowadays that would be pollution. You could take it with you when you next go on a long trip or ask someone you know and trust to take it on their travels. Say: *'I send you away, be gone from my life.'* Leave the doll in that far-off place.

Killing curses

I am most certainly not advising anyone to perform a 'killing curse' or even one that causes grievous bodily harm, but for purely information purposes here are a few from historical sources – although do bear in mind that none of these sources are nowadays considered to be unquestionably accurate. First, from the confession under examination of Elizabeth Sowtherns, alias Demdike, in the 17th century Pendle witch trials, in Lancaster, taken from *Discovery of Witches*, by Thomas Potts:

This Examinate confesseth, and sayth, that the speediest way to take a mans life away by Witchcraft, is to make a Picture of Clay, like vnto the shape of the person whom they meane to kill, & dry it thorowly: and when they would haue them to be ill in any one place more then an other; then take a Thorne or Pinne, and pricke it in that part of the Picture you would so haue to be ill: and when you would haue any part of the Body to consume away, then take that part of the Picture, and burne it. And when they would haue the whole body to consume away, then take the remnant of the sayd Picture, and burne it: and so therevpon by that meanes, the body shall die.

There is a description of poppet curses designed to kill or maim the victim in *The Golden Bough*, by Sir James Frazer.

Perhaps the most familiar application of the principle that like produces like is the attempt which has been made by many peoples in many ages to injure or destroy an enemy by injuring or destroying an image of him, in the belief that, just as the image suffers, so does the man, and that when it perishes he must die... The Peruvian Indians moulded images of fat mixed with grain to imitate the persons whom they disliked or feared, and then burned the effigy on the road where the intended victim was to pass. This they called burning his soul.

A Malay charm of the same sort is as follows. Take parings of nails, hair, eyebrows, spittle, and so forth of your intended victim, enough to represent every part of his person, and then make them up into his likeness with wax from a deserted bees' comb. Scorch the figure slowly by holding it over a lamp every night for seven nights, and say: *'It is not wax that I am scorching, it is the liver, heart, and spleen of So-and-so that I scorch.'*

After the seventh time burn the figure, and your victim will die. This charm obviously combines the principles of homoeopathic and contagious magic; since the image which is made in the likeness of an enemy contains things which once were in contact with him, namely, his nails, hair, and spittle. Another form of the Malay charm...is to make a corpse of wax from an empty bees' comb and of the length of a footstep; then pierce the eye of the image, and your enemy is blind; pierce the stomach, and he is sick; pierce the head, and his head aches; pierce the breast, and his breast will suffer. If you would kill him outright, transfix the image from the head downwards; enshroud it as you would a corpse; pray over it as if you were praying over the dead; then bury it in the middle of a path where your victim will be sure to step over it. In order that his blood may not be on your head, you should say: *'It is not I who am burying him, it is Gabriel who is burying him.'*

Thus the guilt of the murder will be laid on the shoulders of the archangel Gabriel, who is a great deal better able to bear it than you are.

The poem Sister Helen by Dante Gabriel Rossetti tells the tale of a woman killing a man over three days by melting a waxen image. It starts:

'Why did you melt your waxen man
Sister Helen?
To-day is the third since you began.'

'The time was long, yet the time ran,
Little brother.'
(O Mother, Mary Mother,
Three days to-day, between Hell and Heaven!)

Folklorist Edward Lovett in his 1914 exhibition of folkloric and magic dolls in Cardiff, described a practice from Belgium. A doll was made of wax into which pins and nails were inserted into the non-vital parts to bring about pain in the corresponding areas. He said: 'In cases where the victim's death was sought it was placed in a chimney and the doll melted.'

Practical exercise

Devise a poppet spell of your own using assertive magic, in which everyone wins and no one is harmed.

Chapter 9

Decommissioning Poppets

If a poppet or magical doll you have created and enchanted has done all you want it to do, or you wish to discontinue the magical connection between it and a person it represents for any reason, you should conduct a ritual to thank it, then cut the ties and connections. You can also lay the doll to rest or recycle it.

Cast a circle and invite in the elements and any spirits or deities that were present when the doll was enchanted. Thank the doll and state that its work is over. Say: *'I thank you XXX. Your work is done.'*

Pass an athame or scissors around the doll, symbolically cutting any magical, spiritual or energetic ties that connect it to anyone or anything. Say: *'I cut the ties that bound and connected you to XXX.'*

If your magical doll was named, then say: *'I rename you 'doll'. You are as you once were; a thing of [cloth, wax, clay, wood etc]. So mote it be it.'*

If you are intending to keep the doll or repurpose it for other magic, you should then cleanse it with salty water, the smoke of burning herbs or incense, or by the light of the sun or moon. Say: *'You are cleansed of all influence.'*

However, if your doll or poppet was purely created for one specific spell, it is best to recycle it, lay it to rest or destroy it. The way you do that depends on what it is made out of. Take the doll to pieces in the reverse order to how you created it. You can unpick stitches in wool or cloth and untie any threads or cords. Wax or clay that isn't permanently hardened can be kneaded back into a ball. Some dolls would have to be cut up or broken.

Then end your ritual and open your circle. If you are an experienced witch, you probably have your own ways of doing that, but you can simply say: *'The rite is ended, the circle is open.'*

If you are disposing of your doll, please do it in an environmentally friendly way. Natural fabrics, untreated wood or natural unbaked clay can be buried in the soil in your garden to decompose; wax can be melted; some materials can be burnt. Throwing things into running water was one traditional way of disposing of magical items that were no longer to be used, but today that is littering and could land you with a fine as well as polluting the waterway. Also, don't pour anything down the drain that could block it, such as melted wax. You can put doll pieces into the recycling.

Lost and Found

What do you do if you accidentally lose a poppet or magical doll? Well, if you have exhausted all avenues of trying to find it, decommission the doll and make another if you still need one. Do the ritual to decommission a poppet just described, but visualise or imagine the poppet in place of having the real thing. Go through the motions of cutting around the edge of your 'imaginary' doll and then breaking it or cutting it up.

The person the doll represented should cleanse themselves by having a bath to which a little salt has been added and visualising all connections to the doll being cut.

The other question is, what do you do if you find a poppet someone else has made that represents yourself, but you don't want the magic to continue? I have heard of people leaving little poppets with pins in them on people's doorsteps. Usually this is just done to scare the person. If they really wanted to do them harm with a poppet, they probably wouldn't leave it lying around, but there are spells in some magical traditions that involve ensuring the victim of a curse finds the doll.

If you do want to end a poppet spell someone else has cast, you can still go through the ritual to decommission a poppet. You should also have a bath with a little salt added and visualise cutting any remaining ties to the poppet and to the person who attempted to curse you. You might want to leave out the bit about thanking the doll though.

Chapter 10

Deities and Creatures from Myth and Legend

The earliest figurines were quite possibly representations of Goddesses. They are found all over Europe and include the Venus of Willendorf – an 11.1cm carving estimated to have been made between 28,000 and 25,000 BCE. These forms of prehistoric art are called Venus figurines and some people believe they represent a universal Mother Goddess. Most figures are carved from antler, bone or soft stone although others are modelled from clay, such as the Venus of Dolní Věstonice.

Make a Goddess Figurine

Have a search online or in museums and study how the ancient Venus figurines were formed. You could then have a go at making one yourself – either a faithful replica or a modern variation – to put on your own altar to represent the Goddess. You could then fashion a male consort for the Goddess in a similar way, but with male features and, perhaps, antlers to represent the Horned God.

You can, of course, try your hand at shaping a figurative representation of any other deity, mythological being or creature from folklore and legend. Below is a guided visualisation to help you gain inspiration. Make sure you have drawing, painting, sculpting or other crafting materials ready before you do this visualisation, because when it is finished you will start to make your own work of art.

Guided visualisation

It is best to record this guided visualisation first, perhaps on your phone, then play it back and listen to it with your eyes closed. Find a safe and comfortable place, preferably sitting or lying down, then listen to your recording. Be aware that you might need to pause your recording as you do the visualisation unless you have left long gaps between each paragraph in which to fully imagine each stage.

Close your eyes, relax and take three deep breaths in and out. Let your thoughts of the world around you fade away.

Visualise that you are in front of large and impressive wrought metal gates that stand at the entrance to a beautiful park. Look at the gate and visualise it as strongly as you can. Immediately in front of the gate, through the wrought metalwork, you can see a path leading to a lawn. In the distance, on the three sides of the lawn, are gardens of flowers, copses and groves of trees and a gentle meadow leading down to the edge of the water. Look through the gate and visualise the path and this beautiful parkland. Spend some time doing this.

When you are ready, visualise opening the gate.

Walk through, take the path and go across the lawn. You see that ahead of you the path splits into three – one route leading to the gardens of flowers, one to the copses and groves of trees, and one across the meadow down to the edge of the water. Decide which route you will take.

When you have picked your path, you start to walk again, along your chosen route.

As you walk, you notice that at your chosen destination – the gardens, trees or water's edge – there are statues, shrines, pergolas and grottos. These become more obvious as you continue along the path and reach the part of the park you were heading towards.

After a while you reach your destination. Although the path continues into the gardens, trees and along the water's edge, you are free to explore as you will – stay on your path or leave it and wander through the gardens, groves or along the bank.

Look at what's around you, including the greenery and landscape. As you do so, your eyes are drawn to the statues, shrines or other structures. You realise that the statues are of Gods, Goddesses, venerated beings, creatures and people from folklore and mythology – and also wise and respected ancestors and teachers. In the shrines there are icons and images, and in the pergolas, grottos and other small manmade structures there are all sorts of works of art, from sculptures to frescoes, depicting many different deities, archetypes and those worthy of respect.

Wander among them and look at them until you find one you are particularly drawn to. When you do find one that you are interested in, go up to it and study it.

Walk around it and spend as long as you need studying your chosen work of art from all angles...

After a while, when you have studied the work of art, you feel inspired to draw, paint, sculpt or otherwise craft something that relates to it. Perhaps you want to sketch or paint it as it is, perhaps you want to mould a small version from clay, perhaps you feel an urge to carve wood or stone into something like it. It might not be an exact replica, but you hope to capture the essence of it in some way or to create something entirely new, but inspired by it.

Glancing to one side you notice that all the materials you need to create your own work of art have been set out for you. Use them as you will and create your own work of art, based on the masterpiece you have been studying. Take enough time to do this.

When you are finished, you realise it is time to leave the park. Put your art materials to one side but – if you want – you can take the work of art you created with you.

When you are ready, return back the way you came.

Retrace your steps, go along the path and cross the lawn to the gates. Know that even though you will leave the park and the artwork within it, you can take your inspiration for your own work of art with you when you leave. With that knowledge, open the gate again and walk through it out of the park.

As you close the gate behind you, your visualisation of it fades and you return to the normal world.

Wriggle your fingers and toes, take a deep breath, and open your eyes.

If you are lying down, sit up, then use drawing, painting or crafting materials to try to reproduce the work of art you created in the visualisation. It doesn't have to be perfect – it could just be initial sketches. You can return to this as often as you like, perfecting your creation. You can also repeat the visualisation to get more inspiration.

When your work is finished, you can use it as an item of veneration or meditation in your spiritual practice or keep it where it will inspire you in your daily life.

Chapter 11

Dolls of the Dead

Haunted dolls, or normally inanimate objects possessed by some evil entity, are as much a trope in horror tales as Voodoo dolls – and the common understanding is just as inaccurate. Sure, it makes a good scary story, but the reality is far different. In this chapter I'm going to look at three ways in which dolls are associated with the dead: spirit attachments, spirit houses and dolls of remembrance.

Spirit Attachments

First, forget the term 'possessed doll'. The correct term is 'spirit attachment', according to Jayne Harris and Dan Weatherer in their book *What Dwells Within: A Study of Spirit Attachment*. However, Jayne and Dan are convinced that sometimes the spirits of those who have died can become attached to inanimate objects, as they state:

> What is spirit attachment if not the very definition of a haunting? It is believed that ghosts haunt areas that the deceased were either fond of or met their demise within, and there are countless volumes dedicated to the documentation of haunted places and the history behind each alleged ghost... If a spirit can attach itself to a place that it once shared a connection with, then why not an object?

Dolls were what originally interested Jayne and for many years she ran a service called Haunted Dolls through which she bought, researched and then sold ones with spirit attachments. She said most spirits are not dark; they are simply people who have chosen to remain on the earthly plane after death. They do not wish to harm people, they just want to continue to experience the world or to watch over people they are fond of.

If you think a doll you own might have a spirit attachment, you should research its history and make notes of any unusual activity that happens around it. If you wish to try to communicate with the spirit, one way is to cast a circle and then use a pendulum to try to get answers to yes or no questions. Hold the pendulum loosely on its string or chain and work out the motions that mean no and yes by asking questions for which you already know the answer. Then move on to questions you don't know the answers to. When you have finished, thank the spirit and say you wish to end the communication, then open the circle.

Spirit Houses

Spirit houses are effigies in which a spirit is deliberately placed and possibly bound, rather than a spirit choosing to take residence there or becoming attached. In some of the very earliest examples of effigy magic, figures were made of those who had died and then pinned so that their spirits wouldn't rise from the grave to haunt the living. In some cultures, spirits of ancestors were deliberately bound into effigies so they could be venerated. According to the folklorist Edward Lovett in *Handbook to the Exhibition of the Lovett Collection of Dolls, 1914*:

In Central Africa, spirit dolls of the Achewa tribe consisted of a few short pieces of wood bound together with fabric into the figure of a child's doll, the rag being fastened by bark rope.

Inside the fabric is a box made from the handle of a gourd cup. This contains the spirit of a dead ancestor, which has been captured and put into its abode as an item of religious regard. Among the Achewa and Bantu tribes, the spirits of the dead are the object of worship.

I hope no one will be too disappointed that I'm not going to be offering any techniques for binding dead relatives into dolls. *Pagan Portals: Poppets and Magical Dolls* is a beginners' book and this is a pretty advanced topic.

Dolls of Remembrance

Edward Lovett also mentioned that in 1836 some boys found coffin-like boxes each containing a small doll in a concealed cave on Arthur's Seat, Edinburgh. He said similar boxes had been discovered in Germany and Brittany. There the folklore was that if a sailor was lost at sea and the body not recovered, a small doll or cross was made to represent the person, put in a box and a service for the dead performed over it. Those dolls were all put into one place, usually under the effigy of Saint Nicholas – the patron saint of seamen as well as famed for giving toys to children at Yule.

Even today, a doll can be a wonderful way to remember and honour a loved one who has passed on. If possible, use clothing and other items that belonged to them to make either the entire doll or its clothing. If you have a lock of their hair – or just a strand or two from their comb or hairbrush, include that in the doll. You can adorn it with jewellery or other small trinkets that belonged to them.

Put your doll somewhere special. This could be your altar, a shrine you have created for them, their favourite chair or on a shelf. Honour the doll as you desire. You can put fresh flowers there or light a candle (but don't leave candles unattended). The doll can represent your ancestor in rites and rituals, or you can talk to it and visualise talking to your departed loved one. Some people find this helps them get through the natural grieving process and it can also act as a focus if you wish to communicate with the spirit of the person who has passed.

You can also create dolls of remembrance to honour and remember those who died long ago. Although you are unlikely to have personal effects to incorporate in the doll, you can choose colours that are appropriate for them and, if you wish, write or embroider their name.

Artist and performer Denise Rowe created an installation to honour and remember the wise women – and men – who were persecuted during the witch hunts of early modern Europe. In 2016, she invited people to make simple dolls from scraps of red fabric in honour of those who died after being accused of witchcraft. The dolls were to be installed in the landscape when Denise had collected at least a million of them.

Practical Exercise: Make a Doll to Remember those Persecuted for Witchcraft

Here are the instructions Denise Rowe gave to make a doll for the art installation:

Take a roughly hand/palm sized piece of fabric, ideally in shades of red. Gather her up in the middle and tie a strip of fabric, ribbon, wool etc around her. Add a loop to suspend her from a tree.

She also invited completed dolls to be sent to her. For more information, visit the website: www.earthdances.co.uk/dolls/ 4581452555.

Chapter 12

Seasonal Dolls of the British Isles

Dolls and effigies play an important role in the seasonal year in many countries, but here are some of the ways they are incorporated into festivals and celebrations in the UK.

Brigid's Feast Day and Imbolc

In some parts of Ireland and Scotland it is traditional to parade a doll representing St Brigid around the town on January 31, the eve of St Brigid's Feast Day. This doll is given place of honour while everyone taking part in the festivities has a bit of a party, then she is put to bed before being greeted again in the morning. According to folklore, this would bring blessings upon the household for the coming year and clothes left by the doll overnight would also be blessed to help protect those who wore them.

For Pagans, the Goddess Brigid is celebrated in a similar way at the festival of Imbolc on February 1 – although most pagans I know parade the Brigid doll around their house rather than around the town, then put her on their altar and light a candle to honour her. The doll, known as a Brídeóg (also called a 'Breedhoge' or 'Biddy'), is often made from rushes, reeds or straw. You can use the instructions for straw dolls from chapter 3. The doll should be dressed in white cloth and can be decorated with shells or flowers. For many pagans, Brigid is the bride of spring. Her arrival at Imbolc coincides with the first signs of green shoots growing in the soil and perhaps a few snowdrops starting to bloom.

Scarecrows: Springtime Guardians of the Fields

Although scarecrows normally appear in fields and gardens

in springtime – constructed by farmers and gardeners to keep crows from eating newly-planted seeds – as creatures from horror stories they are sometimes associated with harvest-time and Samhain (or Halloween). One possible reason for this is that they look similar to Halloween Jack O'Lanterns. To be honest, I have always wondered whether scarecrows are more effective at scaring off human trespassers than the avian variety.

Today, most farmers use reflective strips of plastic that shimmer in sunlight to deter birds and in the past many would simply shoot the offending crows then hang the corpses from a pole or tree as an example to others. This is probably what Robinson Crusoe meant, in the 1719 novel by Daniel Defoe, when he said: 'I could never see a bird near the place as long as my scarecrows hung there.' Robinson Crusoe is the first known English story to use the term scarecrow, although they were probably used to protect fields for countless years before that. Many villages in the UK have scarecrow festivals, such as the Wray Village Scarecrow Festival, in April. These usually include competitions for the best or most original scarecrow.

Lammas to Harvest's End: Corn Dollies, Straw Dogs and the Bikko

Corn dollies, sometimes called corn mothers, have been made out of straw as part of harvest customs all over Europe for centuries. According to folk legends, the spirit of the corn lives among the crop, but is made homeless by the harvest. James Frazer said in *The Golden Bough* that it was often the very last sheaf of the harvest that was made into a corn dolly. The dolly would have a hollow enclosure within it for the corn spirit to reside during the winter. In the spring, the corn dolly would be ploughed into the first furrow of the field to return the spirit to the land.

Some modern pagans also make corn dollies to put on their altars at Lammas, the festival at the start of the harvest. Traditional corn dollies can be quite complex to make as they involve patterns of twisted, spiralling corn. However, you can make a simple corn loop by plaiting three or four strands of corn, twisting this into a loop and tying the ends. In the spring, you can return it to the garden when the soil is ready to plant seeds.

A less popular harvest doll is the straw dog, which was something no farmer on Orkney wanted to own as it was the booby prize for being slow to get the crops in. The straw dog, or 'bikko', was usually put in a prominent position on the farm building – or 'steedeen' – in secret during the night by the farmer's 'friends'.

Bonfire Night: Guys

November 5 is Bonfire Night in England. Traditionally the days leading up to it were a time for collecting wood for a fire and making a Guy to go on top out of old clothes stitched together and stuffed with newspaper. The Guy's head – in the days before you could easily buy plastic masks – was usually made out of papier-mâché, painted with gruesome features and topped with some unwanted hat. He was crude and basic, but also fun and individual.

The Guy was usually meant to represent Guy Fawkes. Bonfire Night, otherwise known as Guy Fawkes Night, celebrates the foiling of the Gunpowder Plot terrorist attack to blow up the Houses of Parliament on November 5, 1605. Guy Fawkes, a mercenary hired by Catholic conspirators to handle the explosives, was discovered and executed along with his fellow plotters. Burning the image of a man with a moustache and a tall hat to represent Guy on November 5 became the custom. My childhood friends were more likely to make one of a much-hated teacher from school than something looking like Guy Fawkes. We would joyfully watch our effigy go up in flames on November 5 while singing a traditional Bonfire Night song:

Build a bonfire, build a bonfire

Put the teachers on the top
Put the schoolbooks in the middle
And burn the blooming lot!

As I got older, hated teachers were replaced with unpopular politicians, destined for the top of the pyre. These days, however, I would be more wary of making a Guy in the image of any real, living person. It seems a bit too much like real magic rather than just a bit of fun.

Hallowe'en: Jack o Lanterns

Jack o Lanterns might not exactly be dolls, but they are effigies, so I've included them here. Pumpkin lanterns seem as much a part of Halloween as ghosties and ghoulies and things that go bump in the night, but when I was a kid pumpkins weren't easily available in England. That isn't to say we didn't make Halloween lanterns, but instead of hollowing out pumpkins, we carved them out of turnips. From bitter memory I can tell you turnips are the toughest vegetables to carve. You have to hack at them with sharp implements, brute force and the determination of a horror-movie psycho-killer – and even then the resulting lantern is usually best described as malformed. But, when it comes to Halloween lanterns, malformed is probably good. The idea behind them is that by putting a monstrous face in your window or on your doorstep you will ward off any supernatural nasties, because they would not wish to go near anything that looked uglier than themselves.

An old name for an illuminated vegetable is Jack O'Lantern, supposedly named after an Irish trickster called Stingy Jack who managed to con the Devil into paying for his drinks. The Devil, outraged at being fooled, refused to let Jack into hell after he had died, leaving him to wander the Earth in darkness for eternity with only a single coal to light his way.

In parts of Somerset, Jack O'Lanterns are called Punkies, and

Punkie Night is celebrated on the last Thursday of October. Like Halloween, on Punkie Night, children go from door to door in a tradition similar to Trick or Treat. They carry around Punkies made from hollowed out mangel-wurzels – a large root vegetable used as cattle feed – and demand gifts with the rhyme:

It's Punkie Night tonight
It's Punkie Night tonight
Adam and Eve would not believe
It's Punkie Night tonight
Give me a candle, give me light
If you haven't a candle, a penny's all right.
It's Punkie Night tonight.

Yule Tree Fairies

The bringing of greenery into the home is an old tradition for the time around the Midwinter Solstice on December 21, probably dating back to ancient pagan times. However, the decorating of Yule or Christmas trees didn't start until the 15th or 16th century in Germany and Scandinavia. At first things like biscuits were hung from the trees, but decorations grew more elaborate. The tree-topper came later, but was originally a star – a Christian symbol for the star of Bethlehem. Angel dolls as treetoppers generally represented Gabriel, the messenger of God in the Christmas story. In the UK, decorated fir trees only became popular in Victorian times. Pictures of Queen Victoria's Christmas tree, complete with angel doll, appeared in newspapers and started a trend. In England, the male angel tree-toppers developed in the 20th century into a passion for female fairy dolls, which reached a peak around the 1950s, 60s and 70s. Many Pagans still prefer to have a fairy on the top of a Christmas tree as this seems, well, a bit more pagan. According to *History of the Christmas Fairy Doll* by Susan Brewer, an old folkloric belief was that fairies slept in holly during the winter months. Holly has a long history of being used to decorate homes for the winter festival, presumably bringing fairies with it. However, as Susan Brewer points out, fairies were originally considered dangerous. In Victorian times good fairies started to prevail over bad ones and the Victorians very much associated them with Christmas. In pantomimes, it was usually the good fairy or fairy godmother who helped the heroes defeat the villain.

One idea is that Yule tree decorations, as well as looking bright and cheerful at the darkest time of the year, act as magical protection. Anything wishing to cause trouble around the home would be attracted by the shiny trinkets dangling from the tree, which would take their attention away from the mischief they had in mind. A fairy on the top could be considered the ultimate guardian overseeing this magic, sprinkling a little fairy dust with her wand to delight those celebrating the midwinter festival, and deter those who would spoil the party.

Practical Magic: How to Make a Yule Tree Fairy

Here is one way to make your own fairy Yule tree topper. Take a medium-sized wooden spoon. Glue two arms out of pipe-cleaners 2cm below the head (the spoon's bowl). Twist them back to form small looped hands. Cover the head with some glue and, picking a suitable colour for skin-tone, wrap wool around the arms and head to create a uniform appearance.

Make a cone of cardboard that is longer than the rest of the handle. Cut a little hole at the pointy end and put the spoon handle into it, gluing it in place below the arms.

Get a long strip of fabric for the fairy's dress – shimmery netting, stiff lace or organza work well, but you might need to form a petticoat too if it is very transparent. Loosely wrap the fabric around the doll and tie it in place around the waist, leaving a little bunched above the waist for a bodice. Cut a pair of fairy wings from silvery card or stiff netting. Make two small holes in the wings at waist level. Thread ribbon through the two holes and around the waist and tie a reasonably tight bow to hold the wings in place and further secure the dress.

Make a fairy wand from a sparkly silver pipe-cleaner. Put this through one of the hand loops. Attach bunches of wool tied in the middle to the top of the head as hair, then wrap more sparkly silver pipe-cleaner around the head to form a crown. Cut eyes and a mouth out of felt and stick these in place. Stick on extra sparkles, glitter and beads for finishing touches.

Chapter 13

Doll Magic around the World

Every culture around the world has folklore relating to dolls and effigies – even if, as in Islamic culture, there is a belief that lifelike portrayals of animate beings, especially humans, should be avoided because they are potentially powerful distractions.

I do not have space in this small book to cover every aspect of doll folklore and magic worldwide, but I do feel I should mention some important ones. These details are for information and comparison purposes and to offer suggestions for further research. You should always be sensitive to the wishes of people from indigenous and minority cultures and try to avoid causing offense through using elements from those cultures inappropriately.

New Orleans Voodoo and Haitian Vodou

No book about poppets and magical dolls would be complete without a look at the history of Voodoo dolls in relation to New Orleans Voodoo, its background and the cultural collision of European folk magic and African practices. Dr Louise Fenton of the University of Wolverhampton, who curated an exhibition called Poppets, Pins and Power in 2017 at the Museum of Witchcraft and Magic in Cornwall, gave a talk at its annual conference that year, called Cultural Confusion Between Witchcraft and Voodoo. Dr Fenton had been researching the representation of Voodoo for 20 years in an academic context.

On the subject of Haitian magic, she said it is believed slaves taken to Haiti either brought fetishes made of wood or clay with them or made them afterwards. The death penalty was a possibility if a slave was found with one of these, so it is possible that cloth dolls started at that point. Poppet magic was made popular in New Orleans after the Civil War, but there are disagreements about the use of poppets historically in that region. There is not much evidence of poppet use in Haiti, but there is in New Orleans. In 1865 plantation owners went to Louisiana with slaves and Haitian Voodoo came to New Orleans; there was a huge mix of cultures and Voodoo changed a lot at that point. A greater awareness of image magic worldwide was brought about by the 1890 publication of *The Golden Bough*.

Bocio are carved wooden images from Africa that are connected with magic and supernatural beings. They were used as African magic merged with European and were traditionally designed to be mediators with the spirit world – both positive and negative. Voodoo dolls started in New Orleans in the late 19th century. With both artistic and cultural collision, poppets and bocio merged into Voodoo dolls. This is still being practised today.

The 'Voodoo doll' concept became popularised through media such as William Seabrook's *The Magic Island*, published in 1929, which gave a vivid account of Voodoo in Haiti. It was a very racist book, but much of this was lifted and used in the movie White Zombie starring Bela Lugosi. Lafcadio Hearn actually wrote the first zombie novel, but many others followed – usually very inaccurate and offensive. For example, *Cannibal Cousins* by John Craige mentions someone in Haiti finding a doll made in his likeness and in his clothes. He then gets ill. These books sold in their millions and there were also several highly racist films following White Zombie. They perpetuate myths and are cinematic. However, they popularised the use of the Voodoo doll. The words witchcraft and Voodoo started to be used together.

Commercialisation of poppets was unavoidable although for many the emphasis was on making money without understanding the background. You can easily buy poppets for sale today. In New Orleans poppets are sold with Spanish moss hands and feet. There are original dolls in collections. Many from the 20th century are vernacular and of their time. They are often knitted from patterns widely available. The commoditisation of Voodoo dolls in New Orleans has continued. For example, some come with white and black headed pins (and 'made in China' printed on the back). Dolls authentic to New Orleans rarely have pins with them. They are often made of papier-mâché and Spanish moss with not a pin in sight.

At the same conference, Demetrius Lacroix, an initiate of Haitian Vodou, Brazilian Quimbanda and Santeria and a specialist on misunderstood cultures, gave a talk entitled Haitian Vodou Cursing. He explained that Vodou is a combination of family traditions from Africa that were brought to the New World. It is about being alive and ways in which people could continue to do their thing in freedom. There is a history of oppression in Haiti. Vodou is the idea that: 'No one will oppress me.'

During times of oppression in Haiti, people who lived in the mountains were hard to get to, but if they were caught they would be mutilated and left to die. If they got back to the mountains, they were thought to have a super connection to magic and to nature. This was the start of secret societies. All these groups have different relations to spirits that allow them to do certain forms of magic. Forms of cursing that started in these groups then disseminated into public knowledge. Priests of Vodou don't really do curses – they work with spirits. The use of dolls for cursing is generally done by non-initiated members of the public.

Demetrius described how in the international cemetery in Haiti there are four trees. There are things nailed to these trees and some are curses intended to make people die. Gede are spirits lost in passage and the Mother of Gede is the owner of these four trees. You could have a doll created from fabric or wax and nail it to a tree and make an offering, perhaps a chicken; offer it to the Mother of Gede, then come back when the person has died. Trees, earth and fire are very powerful. So, putting an object in a tree or burying it in earth is a very powerful thing to do. Demetrius said that there are ways to reverse a curse in this tradition. The main one is to attend a party that the spirits attend and ask them to help you break the curse.

Japanese Folkloric Dolls and Festivals

Dolls have a huge cultural and folkloric significance in Japan. Dolls representing children, the imperial court, warriors, heroes, fairy-tale characters, gods and occasionally demons have a long tradition and are still made today for household shrines, gift-giving and festival celebrations such as Hinamatsuri, the doll festival, or Kodomo no Hi, Children's Day.

Hinamatsuri is observed in Japan on March 3. Platforms covered with a red carpet are used to display a set of ornamental dolls representing the emperor, empress, attendants, and musicians in traditional court dress of the Heian period. The tradition traces its origins to that era and includes a custom called hina-nagashi, or 'doll floating', in which straw hina dolls are set afloat on a boat and sent down a river to the sea to remove troubles or bad spirits. Nowadays, floating objects are considered a menace to fishermen, so the dolls are removed from the water and brought back to temples to be burnt rather than being allowed to drift out to sea. Dolls were also traditionally displayed in houses during the festival, then taken down immediately afterwards as leaving them past March 4 was considered unlucky, particularly with regards to any daughter's chance of marrying.

In Kojiki, the oldest surviving book in Japan (compiled in the year 712), a scarecrow known as Kuebiko is a god. He cannot walk, but his knowledge is vast because he stands in the open and watches everything that happens.

Protective dolls were made for children or grandchildren while others were used in religious ceremonies to take on the sins of anyone who touched them. Hōko were soft dolls given to pregnant women to protect them and their unborn child.

Japanese Teratu Bozu ('sunshine monk') dolls are magical items used as weather talismans – usually to bring sunshine, but sometimes rain if it is needed for crops. These are made from white tissue paper or cloth and hung from the eaves of houses on string.

Another Japanese tradition is Ushi no Kuko Mairi, in which straw dolls are cursed by having nails hammered into them along with prayers to the kami, or nature spirits, for action against a person. It translates as: 'Going to the shrine at the time of the ox at 2am.' This was a time when such things as ill-wishing might be performed. Performing Ushi no Kuko Mairi is still very much frowned upon in Japan.

South American Dolls

After Voodoo dolls, worry dolls are probably the next most well-known magical dolls in popular culture. Sometimes called 'trouble dolls' and, in Spanish, 'Muñeca quitapena', they are small dolls that originate from Guatemala and Mexico and are usually handmade. A Guatemalan legend about the origin of the Muñeca quitapena refers to a Mayan princess, Ixmucane, who was given a gift from the sun God that would let her solve any problem someone was worrying about.

In their original countries the dolls are made of wire, wool and colourful scraps of fabric, then dressed in Mayan costume. Traditionally they are tiny – often only a couple of centimetres tall. The dolls sold outside their original country are often larger and less well constructed – sometimes just made of paper and wool. They are sold in huge numbers as tourist items in Guatemala and Mexico.

Worry dolls can be given to children who are unhappy, the idea being that they tell their doll about their worries, then put the doll under their pillow so it can take away their woes as they sleep. They have sometimes played a role in modern child psychiatry. Some counsellors have offered a worry doll to young clients as an imaginary, trustworthy listener. In that way, it can act as an agent between the child and adults.

Another tradition found in Western Guatemala is that of making dolls to represent San Simon to put on his altars. People ask him for good health, harmony at home, job security and so on. In some areas where he is honoured, people take it in turns to take care of the San Simon doll in their home for a year, starting on November 1. He is often given offerings of cigarettes or alcohol.

In Ecuador, Ano Viejo is a New Year ritual. People make dolls to represent the year just gone using old clothes. They write down on paper the things they want to leave behind – regrets etc – as a mock will. These are either left on the doorstep or pinned to the doll. The dolls are then placed in comical poses. Sometimes masks are made to represent family members and put on the dolls. At midnight the dolls are burnt as a purification ritual and to represent renewal.

Kachina Dolls in Native American Hopi Culture
In Native American Pueblo culture, kachinas are spirits from the underworld that can bring rain and otherwise help the community. These spirits are represented by dancers in important religious ceremonies. In the Hopi tribe, kachina dolls are given to children so they can learn to recognise the different kachinas – of which there are hundreds. The dolls are usually made of wood and brightly painted to represent the costumes worn by the dancers. They are usually created by the children's uncles. They are not toys, but teaching aids and spiritual items.

Corn Husk Dolls in Native American and Hungary
While corn dollies from the British Isles are traditionally made from long stems of wheat or other cereal crops woven into traditional shapes that often don't look like a person, in both

America and Hungary, the husks – or dried leaves – of corn are traditionally turned into dolls. Native American corn husk dolls do not have faces and there are several possible explanations for this. One legend is that the Spirit of Corn, one of the Three Sisters, made a doll out of her husks to entertain children. The doll had a beautiful face and began to spend less time with the children and more time contemplating her own loveliness. As a result of her vanity, the doll's face was taken away.

In Transylvania, Hungary, corn husk dolls symbolise the fertility of the land and its inhabitants. Making them is a tradition still popular in that region.

Russian Matryoshka Dolls

In the first chapter of this book I related a Russian fairy tale about a magical doll, so it seems right to end the book with another Russian doll tradition – the matryoshka doll, or nesting doll. This is a set of wooden dolls of decreasing size placed one inside another. The name 'matryoshka', which literally means 'little matron', is a diminutive form of the Russian female first name 'Matryona'. They are also known as 'babushka dolls', babushka meaning 'grandmother' or 'old woman'. It actually isn't a very old tradition. The first set of Russian nested doll was made in 1890 by Vasily Zvyozdochkin from a design by Sergey Malyutin, a folk crafts painter at Abramtsevo. They were apparently inspired by a doll from Japan.

The outer layer is usually a woman dressed in Russian peasant costume; the figures inside can be of either gender and the smallest is usually a baby. Modern matroyshkas can depict all sorts of things, from fairy tale characters to politicians.

Although this isn't an ancient tradition, the matroyshka doll is used as a metaphor in Jungian psychology for the levels we have within ourselves and in our relationship with societal forces. Understanding those different forces and how they affect us can help us in a quest for personal development and growth, which is often something those within modern pagan witchcraft use their magic to work towards.

Practical Exercise

Research any customs associated with dolls in the area you live.

References

Books

A Kitchen Witch's World of Magical Herbs and Plants; Rachel Patterson (Moon Books)

All Colour Dolls; Kay Desmonde (Octopus)

Buckland's Complete Book of Witchcraft; Raymond Buckland (Llewellyn)

By Spellbook and Candle: Cursing, Hexing, Bottling and Binding; Mélusine Draco (Moon Books)

Cecil Williamson's Book of Witchcraft; Steve Patterson (Troy Books)

Dolls and Toys of Native America; Don and Debra McQuiston (Chronicle Books)

Effigy: Of Graven Image and Holy Idol; Martin Duffy (Three Hands Press)

English Dolls, Effigies & Puppets; Alice K Early (BT Batsford)

Handbook to the Exhibition of the Lovett Collection of Dolls 1914; Edward Lovett (Museum at Cardiff)

History of the Christmas Fairy Doll; Susan Brewer (Virtual Valley)

MyFetch – The Art and Magick of Crafting Poppets and Voodoo Dolls; Terra Lunawolf (Visual Fix Productions)

Of Shadows: One Hundred Objects from the Museum of Witchcraft and Magic; Sara Hannant (Strange Attractor Press)

Pagan Portals – Candle Magic; Lucya Starza (Moon Books)

Russian Fairy Tales; Alexander Afanasyev

The Golden Bough, Sir James Frazer (www.sacred-texts.com)

The Oxford Illustrated History of Magic & Witchcraft; Owen Davies (Oxford University Press)

The Big Book of Dolls; Mabs Tyler (Book Club Associates)

The Book of Mirrors; Luth Adams (Capall Bann Publishing)

The Power of Poppets; Alexis Morrigan (Kindle)

The Splendid Soft Toy Book; Erna Rath (Search Press)

The Voodoo Doll Spellbook; Denise Alvarado (Weiser Books)

The Witch: A History of Fear; Professor Ronald Hutton (Yale University Press)

What Dwells Within: A Study of Spirit Attachment; Jayne Harris and Dan Weatherer (6th Books)

Witchcraft...Into the Wilds; Rachel Patterson (Moon Books)

Voodoo Dolls in Magick and Ritual; Denise Alvarado (Createspace)

Websites

A Bad Witch's Blog: www.badwitch.co.uk

Doll Babies & Poppets by Oseaana: www.youtube.com/watch?v=x1IfP8iQstw

Dolls of Remembrance: www.earthdances.co.uk/dolls/4581452555

Folkloric Dolls of Claudia Six: www.iamsixyouaresix.com/

Online Etymology Dictionary: www.etymonline.com

We think you will also enjoy...

Candle Magic, Lucya Starza

Using candles in simple spells, seasonal rituals and essential craft
techniques.

*...a comprehensive guide on how to use candles for spells,
in rituals and for meditation and divination. It has quickly
become my preferred book for all aspects of candle magic.*
Philip Heselton

978-1-78535-043-6 (Paperback)
978-1-78535-044-3 (e-book)

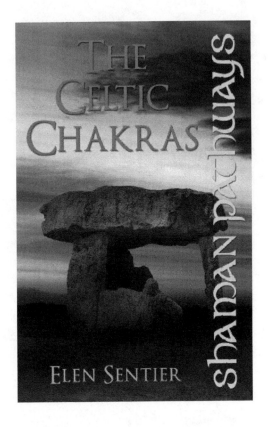

Celtic Chakras, Elen Sentier

Tread the British native shaman's path, explore the Goddess hidden in the ancient stories; walk the Celtic chakra spiral labyrinth.

Rich with personal vision, the book is an interesting exploration of wholeness
Emma Restall Orr

978-1-78099-506-9 (paperback)
978-1-78099-507-6 (e-book)

Best Selling Pagan Portals & Shaman Pathways

Druid Shaman, Danu Forest

A practical guide to Celtic shamanism with exercises and
techniques as well as traditional lore for exploring the Celtic
Otherworld

A sound, practical introduction to a complex and wide-ranging subject
Philip Shallcrass

978-1-78099-615-8 (paperback)
978-1-78099-616-5 (e-book)

Kitchen Witchcraft, Rachel Patterson
Take a glimpse at the workings of a Kitchen Witch and share in
the crafts

*A wonderful little book which will get anyone started on Kitchen
Witchery. Informative, and easy to follow*
Janet Farrar & Gavin Bone

978-1-78099-843-5 (paperback)
978-1-78099-842-8 (e-book)

Best Selling Pagan Portals & Shaman Pathways

Moon Magic, Rachel Patterson
An introduction to working with the phases of the Moon

*...a delightful treasury of lore and spiritual musings that should be
essential to any planetary magic-worker's reading list.*
David Salisbury

978-1-78279-281-9 (paperback)
978-1-78279-282-6 (e-book)

The Awen Alone, Joanna van der Hoeven
An introductory guide for the solitary Druid

Joanna's voice carries the impact and knowledge of the ancestors,
combined with the wisdom of contemporary understanding.
Cat Treadwell

978-1-78279-547-6 (paperback)
978-1-78279-546-9 (e-book)

Best Selling Pagan Portals & Shaman Pathways

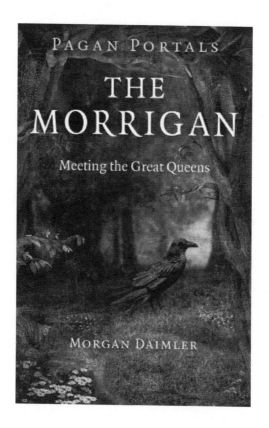

PAGAN PORTALS

THE MORRIGAN

Meeting the Great Queens

MORGAN DAIMLER

The Morrigan, Morgan Daimler

On shadowed wings and in raven's call, meet the ancient Irish
Goddess of war, battle, prophecy, death, sovereignty, and magic

*...a well-researched and heartfelt guide to the Morrigan from a fellow
devotee and priestess*
Stephanie Woodfield

978-1-78279-833-0 (paperback)
978-1-78279-834-7 (e-book)

PAGANISM & SHAMANISM

What is Paganism? A religion, a spirituality, an alternative belief system, nature worship? You can find support for all these definitions (and many more) in dictionaries, encyclopaedias, and text books of religion, but subscribe to any one and the truth will evade you. Above all Paganism is a creative pursuit, an encounter with reality, an exploration of meaning and an expression of the soul. Druids, Heathens, Wiccans and others, all contribute their insights and literary riches to the Pagan tradition. Moon Books invites you to begin or to deepen your own encounter, right here, right now.

If you have enjoyed this book, why not tell other readers by posting a review on your preferred book site. Recent bestsellers from Moon Books are:

Journey to the Dark Goddess
How to Return to Your Soul
Jane Meredith
Discover the powerful secrets of the Dark Goddess and transform your depression, grief and pain into healing and integration.
Paperback: 978-1-84694-677-6 ebook: 978-1-78099-223-5

Shaman Pathways – The Druid Shaman
Exploring the Celtic Otherworld
Danu Forest
A practical guide to Celtic shamanism with exercises and techniques as well as traditional lore for exploring the Celtic Otherworld.
Paperback: 978-1-78099-615-8 ebook: 978-1-78099-616-5

Traditional Witchcraft for the Woods and Forests
A Witch's Guide to the Woodland with Guided Meditations and Pathworking
Melusine Draco
A Witch's guide to walking alone in the woods, with guided meditations and pathworking.
Paperback: 978-1-84694-803-9 ebook: 978-1-84694-804-6

Wild Earth, Wild Soul
A Manual for an Ecstatic Culture
Bill Pfeiffer
Imagine a nature-based culture so alive and so connected, spreading like wildfire. This book is the first flame…
Paperback: 978-1-78099-187-0 ebook: 978-1-78099-188-7

Naming the Goddess
Trevor Greenfield
Naming the Goddess is written by over eighty adherents and scholars of Goddess and Goddess Spirituality.
Paperback: 978-1-78279-476-9 ebook: 978-1-78279-475-2

Shapeshifting into Higher Consciousness
Heal and Transform Yourself and Our World with Ancient
Shamanic and Modern Methods
Llyn Roberts
Ancient and modern methods that you can use every day to
transform yourself and make a positive difference in the world.
Paperback: 978-1-84694-843-5 ebook: 978-1-84694-844-2

Readers of ebooks can buy or view any of these bestsellers by
clicking on the live link in the title. Most titles are published in
paperback and as an ebook. Paperbacks are available in traditional
bookshops. Both print and ebook formats are available online.

Find more titles and sign up to our readers' newsletter at
http://www.johnhuntpublishing.com/paganism
Follow us on Facebook at https://www.facebook.com/MoonBooks
and Twitter at https://twitter.com/MoonBooksJHP